The Story of the Unknown Warrior

11 November 1920

MICHAEL GAVAGHAN

To Lynn, Louise, Stuart, Emma and Laura

This book is dedicated to the thousands of servicemen from all sides who fell in the Great War and who have no known grave

Published by M and L Publications, Preston, Lancashire.

Published in Great Britain.

ISBN 0 9524464 0 5

Printed by Cambridge University Press

Acknowledgements

THIS book could not have been put together without the assistance of others, to whom I am extremely grateful. When I thought of this book two years ago I never fully appreciated the assistance I would require—how kind people and organisations have been. The list of appreciation is not in any order but it includes all those whose encouragement and time was generously given. A special thanks however, must go to the following, for without their help and kind permission, this book would not have been possible:

The Daily Telegraph; *Daily Mirror*, *The Illustrated London News*; Crown copyright material held in the Public Record Office is reproduced with permission of the Controller of HM Stationery Office (especial thanks to Mr N. Forbes); The Royal Archives (Windsor), by gracious permission of HM the Queen; the Dean and Chapter of Westminster (especially to Dr T. Trowles); and to the Imperial War Museum Staff (especially to Mary Wilkinson, Department of Printed Books and Mr Philip Dutton, Photographic Dept.) whose assistance, guidance and general advice in answering all my queries helped me greatly; *Daily Express*; Rogers, Coleridge & White Ltd.; Ewan MacNaughton Associates; Church of England Record Centre.

Thanks also to: The Western Front Association; The Royal British Legion; Ministry of Defence (Army); *Manchester Evening News*; *Lancashire Evening Post*; *Dover Express*; *Liverpool Echo*; Dover Museum; Stena Sea Link; The Naval Museum (Portsmouth); National Railway Museum, York; and the South African, French and German Embassies. Finally, to Ms M. Choules; Information Office, Commonwealth War Graves Commission; Regimental Headquarters, Grenadier and Coldstream Guards; Royal Artillery Museum, Woolwich; Royal Engineers Museum, Chatham; Liverpool Record Office; Harris Museum and Library, Preston; and *Western Mail*.

Thanks to my family, friends and employers who encouraged me, read the manuscript, and pointed out my many errors; and to my three constant travelling companions to the Western Front for the happy times spent there.

To all the above I owe my thanks, but more especially to Mrs Jean Southworth whose patience and good humour made sense of my manuscripts, and to my daughter Emma Jayne who assisted in preparing them. For the end result, I alone take full responsibility. I have checked, written and confirmed, to the best of my knowledge, the copyright material in this book; any mistakes therefore are entirely unintentional.

This book is written by an unknown about an unknown. I hope I have not done him an injustice.

Michael Gavaghan, Preston.

A soldier of the Great War, known unto God. (Author.)

Contents

List of Illustrations

The Cenotaph, Whitehall, London.
(By kind permission, Imperial War Museum.)

Introduction

Scenes without parallel were witnessed in London.

Vast crowds thronged the streets to watch the passing of the Unknown Warrior to his tomb in the Abbey and the procession, heart stirring in its impressive solemnity, was the prelude to a great pilgrimage, the nation's pilgrimage to the Cenotaph which is the peoples lasting monument, a monument for all.

All classes and all creeds were represented, two kings and four Queens were among the mourners. For once there was complete unity—unity in sorrow and in pride.

Manchester Evening News, *11 November 1920*

SEVENTY-FIVE years ago there occurred an event which was to bring this nation to a standstill. The cotton mills of Lancashire, which would bellow out their constant noise, were for two minutes silenced, as were many others; traffic in Liverpool, Manchester, London and Bristol came to a halt, as it did up and down the country; courts stopped their business; prisoners stood to attention in their cells; the Lutine Bell sounded to commence the two-minute silence for those working in the London Stock Exchange and the City. These events would never again be repeated. More could be listed—individual acts coupled with the great display of a nation's thanks which was to take place at the Cenotaph in Whitehall and the Abbey at Westminster.[1] The first two minute silence was held on 11 November 1919.

They came in their thousands—men who fought in the 'war to end all wars', those who had taken part in the retreat from Mons, the chaotic Battle of Loos, the slaughter of the first day of the Somme and finally the mud of Passchendaele—to pay their respects to a fellow comrade: a man unknown to them, but well known. Also there were the mothers, wives and children of those who gave all. Ex-servicemen came from the three services, because the unknown man was to represent them all.

King George V unveiled the Cenotaph at 11.00 a.m. on 11 November 1920,[2] and stood in silence for two minutes;[3] a silence which was to be observed throughout the country and the empire. The gun carriage that bore the oak coffin containing the body had arrived at the Cenotaph at 10.58 a.m., having left Victoria Station at 9.40 a.m. and passing through crowds of unknown thousands. The King, who had earlier placed a wreath of red roses with bay leaves on the coffin, took up his place behind the gun carriage as the nation's chief mourner, and followed the Unknown Warrior to his final resting place in Westminster Abbey.

The Unknown Warrior was laid to rest in Westminster Abbey on Thursday 11 November 1920 at 11.20 a.m., two years to the day since the signing of the Armistice in a railway carriage in the forest of Compiègne, north of Paris.[4]

Lieutenant John Kipling's grave, St Mary's Advanced Dressing Station, Loos. (Author.)

By the end of the day, over 200,000 had people passed the Cenotaph and had also visited the Unknown Warrior's final resting place at the Abbey to pay their respects, and over 10,000 wreaths were laid at the new, unveiled Cenotaph. The nation mourned; cities, towns and villages, all who had sent their men in their country's hour of need, mourned their passing.

For seventy-five years the warrior has remained unknown: to ensure that he should remain so, this book does not in any way attempt to identify that warrior, nor his rank, regiment or to supply any other information relating to his identity, but, drawing on newspaper reports, the Public Record Office, Kew and records from the Royal Archives, Windsor, the Imperial War Museum and Westminster Abbey, attempts to capture this unique event. Finally, it is appropriate to close this introduction with the words seen so often on so many graves in the military cemeteries in France and Belgium—the inscription by Rudyard Kipling, whose own son was killed in 1915 while serving with the Irish Guards:[5]

A soldier of the Great War
Known unto God.

NOTES

1. Westminster Abbey was consecrated on 28 December 1065 by King Edward and since 1368 has been used for the coronation of every sovereign, with the exceptions of Edward V and Edward VIII. The Abbey holds the tombs of kings and Queens, and memorials to the famous and the great—it was here that the Unknown Warrior was to be buried. The Abbey is under the jurisdiction of the Dean and Chapter, subject only to the sovereign.
2. The Cenotaph was designed by Sir Edwin Lutyens and made of Portland stone.
3. R. Blythe, *The Age Of Illusion* (Oxford University Press, 1983), p. 6. Sir Percy Fitzgerald, a South African, had told Lord Milner that there had been a daily observance in Cape Town all through the war, called the 'two minutes pause as a salute to the dead'. King George V liked this idea, and at 11 o'clock on 11 November 1919 the dancing, the shouting and the spending stopped. Edward Honey an Australian journalist is also credited with the idea.
4. The Armistice was re-signed every thirty days until the Treaty of Versailles in 1919 finally brought the Great War to a close, but laid the foundation for the next one twenty years later. The carriage used was later destroyed in Berlin in the Second World War by the Allied offensive. The Germans had taken it there after the Battle of France in 1940, after making the French sign the surrender documents in the same carriage.
5. The Household Division casualties for 1914–18 were: killed 14,653; wounded 28,398. Over nine million men died in the war of 1914–1918. Great Britain lost 1.66, France 1.28, Germany 1.35.

The original Cenotaph, with flags.
(By kind permission of the Imperial War Museum.)

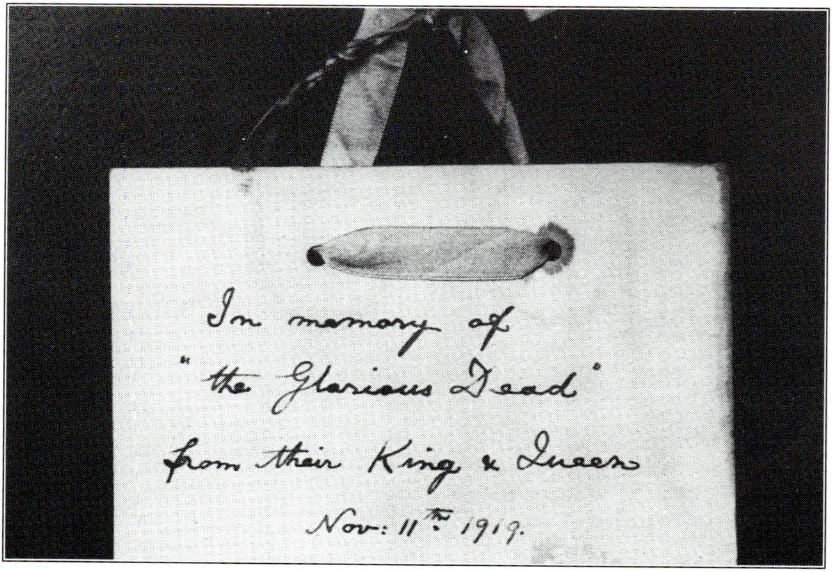

The King and Queen's card, taken from the wreath laid in November 1919.
(By kind permission of the Imperial War Museum.)

Canal Bridge, Mons. Scene of the winning of the first VC by Lieutenant Dease in the Great War. (Author.)

Main Road, Mons. The monument is where L/Cpl Thomas, 4th Royal Dragoons, fired the first British shot of the war. (Author.)

THE CENOTAPH.

PROPOSAL TO FOLLOW FRANCE'S FINE IDEA.

Shall an unnamed British hero be brought from a battlefield in France and buried beneath the cenotaph in Whitehall?

France proposes to honour 1,200,000 dead poilus by burying the body of an anonymous hero in the Pantheon in Paris, and the suggestion is made that the British nation should similarly honour the private soldiers who gave up their lives for their country. The most appropriate spot, it is suggested, is the cenotaph in Whitehall.

The idea yesterday received whole-hearted support in many influential quarters.

"The idea, I confess, is an excellent one, and appeals to me immensely," said the Lord Mayor to a "Daily Express" representative yesterday.

"Anything I can do to further the scheme and help in the arrangements to carry it out I will do gladly, and I am sure all my colleagues will support it heartily.

"I cannot think of a better way of paying homage to the memory of the hundreds of thousands of our gallant dead who lie in France and in more distant lands."

A prominent official of the Peace Celebrations Committee also gave his support to the suggestion.

"The cenotaph is the shrine of a great Empire," he said. "It is a hallowed spot in the heart of the metropolis, and the homage of the British people in all parts of the world crystallises there.

"It is, however, a hollow tomb, but the dust of just one soldier, unknown and undistinguished, would lend it a sacredness worthy of so great a monument."

The cenotaph, as it stands now, is only a temporary structure, but it has been already decided to erect in its place a permanent memorial to our dead.

Who was first?
Daily Express, *16 September 1919.*
(Reproduced by kind permission of the Daily Express.*)*

I

The Beginning

'It was a great idea—in fact an inspiration,' said an English working man, and many others have said the same. 'They say well, for it was.' 'It came to me, it was somehow sent to me'—'I know not how'—in the early part of the year 1916.

The Reverend David Railton MC, MA.[1]

THIS book covers an event which took place seventy-five years ago; an event which from the beginning to the end lasted only five days, yet was approved by the King, supported by the Prime Minister and by an overwhelming majority of the population. Unfortunately, there still remain many conflicting accounts of what happened over those five days. Such was the haste that the planners of the ceremony did not bother with a precise chronicle of the event. Many details were never made public. I have attempted to clarify the situation.

What effect this event had on the nation is now perhaps difficult to understand, but the bringing home of the Unknown Warrior who was to represent all the services was, to many, going to bring the war of 1914-18 to an end—but not necessarily an end to their feelings towards it.

The 'Unknown Warrior' was a new idea—or was it?[2] Indeed, it had only recently been decided that the burial of such a soldier was to coincide with the unveiling of the Cenotaph.[3] The two major questions which perhaps still have to be fully answered are those relating to the number of bodies chosen, and which flag was used during the time the body was moved from France to London.

In considering the first question, that of the bodies, I have relied upon the account of Brigadier General Wyatt, as I have not seen or read any other acceptable account. The question regarding the flag is a more difficult one. Railton's flag, often referred to as 'The Padre's Flag', was used in London and, as we will read, is still there. Some accounts state that this flag was used from the beginning to the end, another that it was a flag which now belongs to the Henfield Branch of the British Legion in Sussex! One newspaper account says that the flag used was the one which also covered the bodies of Nurse Edith Cavell and Captain Charles Fryatt; this could hardly be 'The Padre's Flag'. Railton did ask for his flag to be used on the day, as it had

Grave marked by an inverted rifle, near Combles. (By kind permission of the Imperial War Museum.)

'seen service'. The flag had been given to Railton by his mother-in-law. The Union Flag used at the final selection was not, I believe, Railton's, but his flag was used on 11 November. It was a Union flag taken by HMS *Verdun* which covered the coffin from Boulogne to London. The flag held by the Briish Legion in Henfield could well have been used at the selection. But one of the aspects of researching this book has been those many questions that still have no answer. As I will mention again in the account of the Unknown Warrior, things were done extremely fast, leaving little evidence for posterity.

The initial plan was to unveil the new monument in Whitehall as the nation's premier memorial to those who had died in the service of their country. The idea of the warrior came later. The survivors of that Great War and the people who can remember that November day seventy-five years ago dedicated to the comrades and loved ones lost, are now getting fewer and fewer. But that day, for two minutes united the country, and this one unknown warrior brought people from every section of society in their hundreds of thousands to pay their respects. That November morning the Cenotaph had to share honours with him; but every November the Cenotaph remains the centre of attraction as the country remembers the dead of both wars and later campaigns.

In 1916, a young army padre, the Reverend David Railton, MC (who had won the Military Cross for helping a wounded officer and two private soldiers, whilst under heavy enemy fire), having conducted a burial service was returning to his own billet at Earringham, near Armentières. Here is his account of what he noticed:

> At the back of the billet was a small garden and there six paces from the house was a grave . . . the inscription that was engraved roughly on a plain white, wooden cross, was 'An Unknown Soldier of the Black Watch'.

This was to have a profound effect on Railton who, before the war, had served as a private soldier in the Scottish Territorials and had loved every inch of Scotland. For this single cross—which in the years to come was to multiply by tens of thousands—was the idea out of which the warrior was to come forth. That idea remained with him for the rest of the war. He wrote to Sir Douglas Haig, GOC the British Army in France and Belgium, with the suggestion that a body should be chosen and brought back and buried in England, but unfortunately he received no reply. Railton remained on the Western Front until hostilities ended in 1918.[4]

After the war, Railton was appointed Vicar of St John the Baptist Church at Margate, Kent. In August 1920, he wrote a letter to the Dean of Westminster, the Rt Revd Herbert Ryle, suggesting again the idea which had remained with him since he saw that single grave at Earringham in July 1916. He explained his actions as follows:

> He was worried that the great men of the time might be too busy to be interested in the concerns of a mere padre. He had also thought of writing to the King but was concerned that his advisors might suggest some open space like Trafalgar Square, Hyde Park etc. . . . Then artists would come and no one could tell what weird structure they might devise for a shrine!

'There could be only one true shrine, Railton wrote, and that, if possible should be Westminster Abbey, the Parish Church of the Empire. Although tempted to write to the newspapers, he decided against it, worried that his idea might be taken over and become a stunt![5]

So, in August 1920, at the suggestion of his wife who, having listened to his problem, simply informed him it was to be 'now or never!', he wrote to the Dean of Westminster, the Rt Revd Herbert Ryle, whom he had never met. As Railton was to admit, it was the Dean who overcame all difficulties to ensure that the warrior was buried in the Abbey. A note by Colonel Wigram, the King's Assistant Private Secretary, stated on 3 December 1920 that the suggestion of an Unknown Soldier had been in existence for some time: it was the French who had given us the idea, though they did not put it into practice until later. This can be confirmed by the story in the *Daily Express*, September 1919 (see page 6). The French were to bury their unknown soldier on the same day as the British, theirs being buried under the Arc de Triomphe.

Whether or not Railton's idea started the whole thing off perhaps does not really matter now—he certainly contributed to it. It was also in this letter that the padre suggested the use of his flag, given to him by his mother-in-law, rather than one which had not seen service. Railton's flag was used on the day, to cover the oak casket, containing the Unknown Warrior.

Railton wrote that 'a soldier should be selected from the thousands of those who had no known grave, and be brought back to England to represent all those who fell'. In 1920 there still remained thousands awaiting interment

Seeking a comrade's grave, Pilckem, 22 August 1917.
(By kind permission of the Imperial War Museum.)

in the newly established war cemeteries,[6] and even today the bodies of fallen soldiers are still found on the sites of the battlefields: over 300,000 British and Dominion soldiers have no known grave.[7]

On receipt of Railton's letter, the Dean replied within days: 'I am perhaps not altogether in a position to give you a final decision . . . The idea shall germinate.'[8] In the second week of October the Dean wrote to Railton informing him that he had been in communication with the Prime Minister, the King and the War Office, and that an announcement would be made by the Prime Minister on the afternoon of 19 October.[9] When the Dean received Railton's letter he took up the idea with great enthusiasm and was to play a leading role in bringing the warrior back. He replied:

> Dear Mr Railton
> The idea which you suggested to me in August, I have kept steadily in view ever since. I have been occupied actively upon it for the last two to three weeks. I have necessitated communciations with the War Office, Prime Minister, Cabinet and Buckingham Palace. The announcement which the Prime Minister will, or intends to, make this afternoon, will show how far the government is ready to co-operate. Once more I express my warm acknowledgement and thanks for your letter.

We now follow the course of the letters between Ryle, the Royal Household and Railton in laying the foundations for this unique event. Dean Ryle wrote to Lord Stamfordham, the King's Private Secretary, as follows:

> I am desirous to approach The King upon a matter . . . There are thousands of graves, I am told, of English 'Tommies' who fell at the front—names not known. My idea is that one such body (name not known), should be exhumed and interred in Westminster Abbey, in the Nave.[10]

The King had already agreed to unveil the Cenotaph, after being informed by the Prime Minister that it was the general desire that none other than the King himself should carry out the task, and the ceremony was to take place that November. However, the King made clear that any speeches were to be made by the Prime Minister.[11] It must be stated that the Prime Minister, like everyone else, was deeply affected by the war.

The King's view was given in Stamfordham's reply to the Dean dated 7 October 1920: 'His Majesty is inclined to think that nearly two years after the last shot fired on the battlefields of France and Flanders is so long ago that a funeral now, might be regarded as belated.'[12]

This reply from the palace was disappointing. However, he had (as he mentioned in his letter to the palace) made contact with both the Prime Minister and General Sir Henry Wilson and they had given their support to the plan and greeted it with enthusiasm, as did may others whom he had written to and met. The idea of the Unknown Warrior was, as we shall see, greeted with great enthusiasm, not only by the three services, but by the nation as a whole.

However, it was not that the King had ruled out the possibility, and did not necessarily wish to prevent the idea from taking place. He was fully aware of the public feeling about the war: 'One false move and there would be a morbid side-show in the National Shrine.'[13] He therefore sounded out the views of the Prime Minister who, as we know, was very keen on the idea and convinced the King of its merits. It cannot be denied that the idea, once known, did indeed catch the public's imagination and from the time it was made public, press coverage was to make great play of the occasion.

It should be remembered that between 1919 and 1920 there were upwards of two thousand strikes, and the nation was still returning to peace-time existence. The possibility of employment for those who had done their duty was small, they felt a sense of being let down by those who had promised them that they would return to 'a land fit for heroes', and 'as the second anniversary of the war drew near, a moral and material shabbiness enveloped everything'.[14]. Newspapers in 1920 regularly carried stories calling for more ex-servicemen to be found work (see page 12), and did so for a few years more. In less than ten years we would see a general strike and the start of the Depression.

ARMISTICE WEEK.

Find

JOBS

For EX-SERVICE MEN.

From the Western Mail, *11 November, 1920.*

The wheels of the government began to turn. At a Cabinet meeting held in October it was agreed that a Memorial Service Committee should be formed to organise the selection and burial of a soldier from the war fields of France and Belgium. This committee met on three occasions only. A letter sent to the Dean informed him of the King's approval of his suggestion of 4 October. The letter dated 18 October contained the line: 'It is hoped that the ceremony can be arranged to take place on Armistice Day.'[15] The country was to ensure it did.

Lord Curzon, who at the time was the Foreign Minister, was a strange choice to head the committee as he was not a firm believer in the two minutes' silence.[16] Sir Douglas Dawson (extra equerry to the King) was to be the King's representative. The British Government and people would respond to the occasion as perhaps only the British can.

Brigadier General Wyatt, who was GOC of British troops in France and Flanders, was informed of the idea when he was on an official visit to the old Western Front in his capacity as a director of the War Graves Commission for the War Office. The visit was in July and the then Adjutant General, Sir George MacDonogh, mentioned to him that the Dean had written to him about the selection of a soldier to be sent back and buried at Westminster. He asked Wyatt what he thought of the suggestion and he replied that he thought it was a 'wonderful gesture'.

Why such excitement swept the country is perhaps difficult to understand seventy-five years later. Over 680,000 men had been killed and over two million injured, with many thousands of them crippled. No-one in the country expected such loss when we went to war in 1914—we had, after all, been assured that the boys would be home for Christmas. Now a foreign field was to be the final resting place for many hundreds of thousands. Nearly all were buried near to where they fell, and many thousands more had no grave at all. Those who were wounded on the Western Front and brought home, only to die of their wounds later, were buried here. After the war, many thousands of Tommies who had been buried in temporary cemeteries in France and Belgium were moved to the new military cemeteries. By the 1920s trips were being organised to the Western Front and many thousands made their pilgrimage.[17]

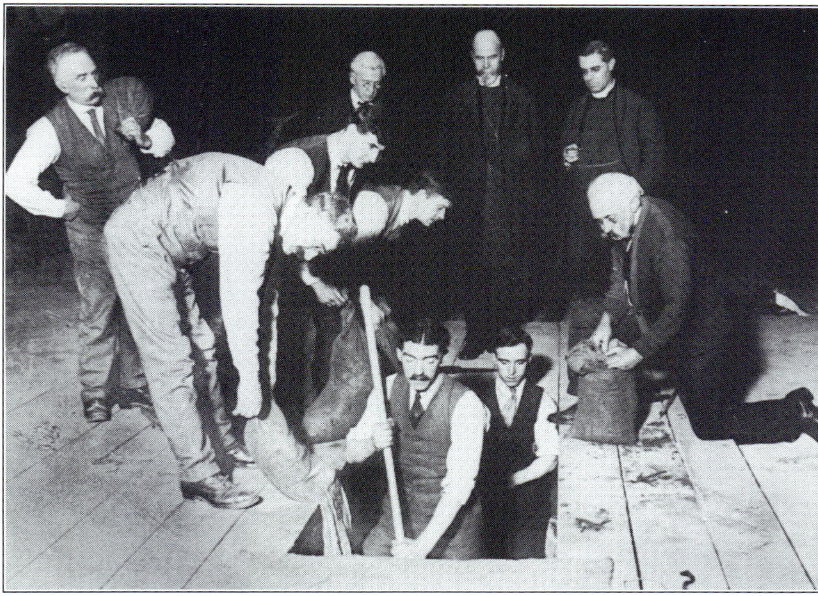

The grave of the Unknown Warrior being prepared at Westminster Abbey. (By kind permission of the Dean and Chapter of Westminster.)

It was perhaps the fact that so many soldiers had no known grave which made this one soldier's home coming more appealing, for here could be somebody's son, brother, husband or father—a loved one who, for many, was at last going to bring an end to their war.

All the pomp and ceremony of the nation began slowly to move. Signals were sent, messages despatched to all the main government departments, making the country ready for the return of its Unknown Warrior. War memorials were to be raised over the ensuing years in every city, town and village giving the names of those who had died for their country and, in time, including the names of those who fell in the Second World War and later campaigns. There would, however, be only one tomb to hold the nation's unknown son. This warrior without rank was to be given a Field Marshal's funeral and all that went with it and, as we shall see, he got even more—a nation's thanks. The authorities made certain it would be dignified, but the whole event was to be overwhelming.

In France, Lt Col Henry Williams received orders which set in motion the selection of the bodies, of which only one would become the 'Unknown Warrior'. Of nothing more could be said than that he did his duty. He was coming home.

NOTES

1. *Our Empire*, Vol. VII, November 1931. Railton was born at Leytonstone, London in 1884 and received his MA at Keble College, Oxford in 1911 and the MC in 1916. During the Second World War he was the Archbishop's Visitor to the RAF, 1943–5.
2. See also *Our Empire* Vol VII, No 8, 1931; Lt. Col. H. Williams' obituary, *The Daily Telegraph*, 14 October 1993; *Daily Express* 16 September 1919.
3. Sir Edwin Lutyens—Designed the Cenotaph (1919–20). He deliberately avoided incorporating a cross in the Cenotaph, because he felt that Indian and Muslim troops in the victory parade would not want to salute a Christian symbol. The same would apply to other religions.
   Sir Reginald Blomfield—Designed the Menin Gate, Ypres and the White Cross of Sacrifice seen in nearly every military cemetery.
   Herbert Baker—Designed the Indian Memorial at Neuve-Chapelle and the memorial to South African troops at Delville Wood.
   Rudyard Kipling selected the inscription 'Their name liveth for ever more' from Ecclesiasticus for the Stone of Remembrance. Headstones in the cemeteries measure 2ft. 6in. high and 1ft. 3ins. wide and are uniform in all military cemeteries.
4. During the war he served as chaplain to the Northumberland Fusiliers, later being transferred to the 141st Infantry Brigade. Appointed Senior Chaplain to the 42nd (London) Division and finally of the 19th (Western) Division.
5. *Our Empire*, Vol VII, No 8, 1931.
6. The Commonwealth War Graves Commission was established by Royal Warrant on 21 May 1917. (Please sign the visitors book when visiting the War Cemeteries.) 'Commonwealth' replaced 'Imperial' in in its title in 1960.
7. At St Mary's Advance Dressing Station Cemetery, Loos, in July 1992, the inscription on the headstone 'an officer of the Irish Guards' was replaced and the new headstone read 'Lieutenant John Kipling, Irish Guards'. He had been found to be the only full lieutenant serving with the Irish Guards killed at Loos that day. He was eighteen when he died. (See photograph page 2). One of the many 'silent cities' as his father Rudyard Kipling, a member of the War Graves Commission, called these cemeteries. Over 90 per cent of those buried in the cemetery are unknown.
8. Railton-Ryle, *Our Empire* Vol. VII, No. 8, 1931.
9. Ryle-Railton, Our Empire, Vol VII, No 8, 1931.
10. RA GV 01637/1, Ryle–Stamfordham, 4 October 1920.
11. RA GV PS 30880, Stamfordham–Davies, 26 September 1920.
12. RA Geo V 01637/2 , Stamfordham–Ryle, 7 October 1920.
13. R. Blythe, *The Age of Illusion* (Oxford University Press, 1983) p. 8.
14. *The Age of Illusion*, p. 7.
15. GOVe 01637/12.
16. *The Age of Illusion*, p. 8.
   The members of the Memorial Service Committee were: Lord Curzon (chair-

man); Lord Lee of Fareham; Mr Churchill; Mr Walter Long; Mr Short; Sir Alfred Mond; Colonel L. Storr (secretary). (CAB 27/99)

17. The United Kingdom still pays over 80 per cent of the cost for the maintenance of the war cemeteries. Australia, Canada, South Africa, New Zealand and India contribute the remainder. Anybody requiring more information about visiting the above should contact the Commonwealth War Graves Commission (address listed at the back of the book).

It was not until the 1960s that the ban on repatriation of service personnel killed in action abroad was lifted, due to the fact that burial places abroad could no longer be guaranteed. It was this ban that made the Warrior's homecoming more poignant.

The coffin of the Unknown Warrior in Westminster Abbey, 7 November 1920, with the Actors' Pall. (By kind permission of the Imperial War Museum.)

2

Selection

THE method of selection was to be simple, and its very simplicity made it impossible that the identity of the soldier could be known. The aim of the whole selection process was to ensure anonymity.

Accounts do vary concerning the way in which the soldier was chosen. According to Herbert Jeans only one grave was selected, in the area of Ypres, from which a body was taken and the grave later filled. John Hundeval, in his article, puts the number at six. Both accounts must be ruled out, as other accounts seem to be more consistent with each other, stating that the body was to be selected from only four areas of main British involvement.[1]. The Imperial War Museum opinion is that the account by Wyatt is perhaps the acceptable one. Brigadier General Wyatt only saw four bodies before him when he entered the temporary chapel at St Pol. An information sheet is available from the Imperial War Museum which attempts to explain this dilemma and suggests that the account by Wyatt is the correct one (held by the Department of Documents). A nurse serving with the QMAAC at St Pol on 7 November observed four funeral cars arriving that day at St Pol. Colonel Gell, who accompanied Wyatt that evening, never queried his account, and during my researches I have found no evidence to the contrary. Most of the accounts were written in the 1920s and, because he felt that many of these were inaccurate, Wyatt decided to put the record straight. Throughout this chapter, therefore, I use Wyatt's account of the selection.

Brigadier General Wyatt, GOC British Forces France and Flanders, received instructions from the War Committee, which he passed on to Lt Col Henry Williams, for the exhumation of four unknown soldiers from the areas of the Somme, Aisne, Arras and Ypres. The parties consisted of four groups, each comprising one officer and two other ranks, armed with a shovel and a sack and driving a field ambulance. On 7 November, on the battlefields which were still marked by thousands of wooden crosses, these groups commenced their tasks, no group knowing the whereabouts of the others. They had been instructed that the body must be taken from a grave which had been marked 'Unknown British Soldier'[2] and that the soldier must have fallen in the early years of the war, to allow nature to cause sufficient deterioration of the body. The parties themselves were not aware of the importance of their selection—the bodies were 'mere bones', according to Wyatt. Such was the haste that correspondence between top and bottom and those removing the bodies is almost non-existent.

The grave of an unknown Canadian soldier, Western Front, October 1916.
(By kind permission of the Imperial War Museum.)

A cemetery in the course of construction, Australian Corps, Gillemont Farm, 3 October 1918.
(By kind permission of the Imperial War Museum.)

The Unknown Warriors of 1920

How One Was Selected for Abbey Burial

From Brig.-Gen. L. J. WYATT
G.O.C. British troops, France and Flanders, 1920, and Director of War Graves Commission

TO THE EDITOR OF THE DAILY TELEGRAPH

SIR—From time to time accounts have been published purporting to relate how and by whom the Unknown Warrior's body was selected in France for burial in Westminster Abbey on November 11th 19 years ago.

In July, 1920, I was making one of my many visits, as G.O.C. of British Troops in France and Flanders as Director of the War Graves Commission, to the War Office to discuss matters with the then Adjutant-General, Sir George Macdonagh. During our talk he said that the Dean of Westminster had been to see him, and had suggested that the body of a British Soldier, whose identity was unknown, should be brought over from France and buried in the Abbey. The Adjutant-General asked what I thought of the idea, and my reply was that I considered it would be a wonderful gesture.

Part of Brigadier General Wyatt's letter to The Daily Telegraph, *November 1939.*

Meanwhile, instructions had already been dispatched by Headquarters Eastern Command on 6 November, concerning the ship which would carry the coffin, the time of her arrival, and that a salute of nineteen guns would be fired.[3] The Admiralty also sent a signal to HMS *Verdun* informing her of departure dates and of the ceremonies which would be carried out in Boulogne and Dover. The signal even included the instruction that HMS *Verdun* was to pay for pilotage at Boulogne, as this was compulsory; a tug was available at the port, supplied by the South Eastern and Chatham Railway Co. Finally, two undertakers, Mr Nodes and Mr Sourbutts, were to be expected, who would be issued with suitable identification and were to be taken to France.[4]

It must be emphasised that much of the procedure was carried out very quickly indeed.[5] There were after all, only three meetings of the Selection Committee and time was short. No fewer than three separate orders had to be issued covering the ceremony at Dover alone.

The bodies selected by each group were placed into sacks and transported by motor ambulance to the Military HQ at St Pol, where they were received by the Rev. George Kendal OBE and again examined to confirm that they were British, and that no name, regiment or other means of identification could be established.[6] All

The cemetery at St-Pol-sur-Ternoise. (Author.)

groups involved in the selection of the bodies arrived at separate times and left immediately so that no group could confer with another, and no-one could know from which area any body came. A guard was then placed at the hut to prevent anyone entering the makeshift chapel where the bodies lay.

At midnight on 7 November, a small group of officers gathered near the hut outside the Military Headquarters at St Pol.[7] Brigadier General Wyatt was informed that the bodies were laid out and that the groups responsible for the selection had gone. Accompanied by Colonel Gell, he passed the guard outside the Nissen hut, and on entering the hastily-made chapel Wyatt saw before him four bodies on stretchers, and the shell of a coffin which had been sent from England the day before and was now placed in front of the altar. Some accounts state that the officer making the selection was blindfolded, but Wyatt himself does not mention being blindfolded and, as the bodies were already hidden by Union Flags which had been laid over all the stretchers, identification was impossible.[8] Both officers knew what was required and carried out their task quickly and in a dignified manner. Wyatt simply touched one covered body, and thus the Unknown Warrior was selected. It was as simple as that.

With the assistance of Colonel Gell they placed the body into the plain deal shell, secured the lid and placed over it a Union Flag. They then both left the chapel, and the guards remained at their post all night to prevent anyone from entering. Sgt Scout, Sgt Stevens and Cpls Strong and Dixon were the British NCOs guarding the body.

Two of the battle areas from which the bodies were selected: Ypres (top) and Somme. (Author.)

German war cemetery at Sailly-sur-Lys, containing five thousand graves. (By kind permission of the Imperial War Museum.)

Inside the cemetery at St-Pol-sur-Ternoise. (Author.)

What happened to the other bodies does remain slightly puzzling. According to Wyatt they were buried in the cemetery at St Pol but, while there are still some unnamed graves in the cemetery of St Pol, I doubt if they are connected to this story. In his letter to the Dean of Westminster of July 1978, Sir Cecil Smith gives a different, and very detailed, account which also confirms Wyatt's statement that only four bodies were selected:

> There was no lack of suitable places in which to deposit the bodies as the area had been fought over . . . There were old trenches running in all directions. The burial party quickly selected a spot and the bodies were quickly transferred. The three bodies were buried in a shell hole on the road to Albert, to which the chaplain added a simple prayer.[9]

It was later reported that three unknown bodies were recovered in that area and re-buried in one of the many new military cemeteries; but, out of many thousands no doubt found there, there is no way of knowing whether these were the same three soldiers.

The following morning chaplains from the Church of England, Roman Catholic and Non-Conformist churches held a service in the makeshift chapel and at noon the body, accompanied by the Rev. George Kendall, was placed into motor ambulance no. 63638 and driven to Boulogne under military escort. According to Wyatt, six barrels of earth accompanied the body 'so that he might lie in the earth so many gave their lives for'.

NOTES

1. See The Daily Telegraph, 14 October 1993, obituaries, Lt. Col H. Williams. I have listed at the back of the book all the articles covering the selection of the Warrior; even now they make interesting reading. The body from the Ypres sector came from Bleuet Farm Cemetery near Elverdinghe.
2. Confirmation was to be by British military uniform.
3. PRO W032/3000 Annex A NO 1
4. See extracts of message, Annex A No 2 PRO W032/3000
5. Brigadier General Wyatt, *The Daily Telegraph*, November 1939: 'In October I received a notification from the War Office that King George V had approved the suggestion and the proposal that the burial should be in Westminster Abbey on 11 November. I issued instructions . . .'
6. Years later there was concern that the bodies had been chosen by French officers. This was not so—they were chosen by British officers only, see *The Daily Telegraph*, Letters to the Editor, 5 April 1972, headed 'The British Unknown Warrior'.
7. Brigadier General Wyatt, *The Daily Telegraph*, 11 November 1939.
8. Brigadier General Wyatt, *The Daily Telegraph*, 11 November 1939.
9. By kind permission Dean and Chapter of Westminster.

The Reverend David Railton. (By kind permission of Mr A. S. Railton.)

King George V holding the helmet of an unknown German warrior.
(By kind permission of the Imperial War Museum.)

3

St Pol–Dover[1]

The Unknown Warrior and his escort party arrived at Boulogne at about 3.00 p.m. on 9 November, having passed through both British and French troops lining the route outside the town. On entering the courtyard of Boulogne-sur-Mer (the old chateau of the Port of Boulogne) the body was received by a group of distinguished guests, among them Colonel Bradstock, Major Fitzsimons, Major Diebold of the French Army and Mr M Labean, Sub-Prefect of the District. The bearers stepped forward and withdrew the coffin from the field ambulance. With it came the earth taken from the fields of Flanders (Railton mentions a hundred sand-bags[2]) which was to be used to cover the body in the grave at Westminster. The coffin was draped by a Union Flag which it is claimed was supplied by Captain Brooks a member of 68 Company of the Graves Registration Unit.

The bearer party, all British or Dominion soldiers, carried the coffin to its temporary resting place in the officers' mess—the library of the chateau—which had been made into Chapel Ardente, and here the Unknown Warrior spent his last night on French soil. The guard to protect this precious soldier was made up of *poilus* from the Boulogne Regiment, which had recently been awarded the Legion of Honour for its service in the war.

The following morning the body—still wrapped in the sack in which it had arrived from St Pol, and inside the coffin shell—was placed into a plain oak coffin which had been brought from England the previous night. Designed and constructed by the British Undertakers' Association, it was made from an oak tree which had stood in the gardens at Hampton Court Palace.[3] A photograph of the coffin was taken in Westminster Abbey, prior to its being sent to France, and this can be seen in chapter 1. It was made secure by wrought iron bands, and on top was laid a Crusader's sword, given by King George V from his own private collection. The inscription carved on the lid in Gothic letters read

A British Warrior Who Fell In The Great War 1914–1918
For King and Country

At 9.30 a.m. on 10 November the Adjutant-General, Lieut Gen. Sir George MacDonogh, gave the order for the coffin to be removed from the chapel to start its journey back to England. The plain oak casket with its valuable cargo was carried by the same bearer party as on the previous day: one sergeant major from the Royal Army Service Corps, one sergeant from the Royal

Engineers, one gunner from the Royal Garrison Artillery, one Australian from the Light Horse, one private from the Canadian Infantry, one private from the 21st Bn London Regiment (1st Surrey Rifles), one private Machine Gun Corps and one private from the Royal Army Medical Corps. It appears that their names were never recorded. It was here that the Union Flag from HMS *Verdun* was used to cover the coffin.

The casket was then placed on the rear of a Royal Army Service Corps wagon, driven by a French soldier and pulled by six black artillery horses. A detachment of the 6th Chasseurs of Lille were drawn up in front of the wagon. On leaving the chateau the cortège, with the eight British and Dominion soldiers marching alongside, slowly made its way to join the main procession formed at the Old toll-bar, known as the 'Denier soue'. The senior British officer, Lieutenant General Sir George MacDonogh, was the King's representative and, accompanied by other British officers, would return with the body to Dover. The French sent a division of all arms with their Colours. Marshal Foch, who arrived by car accompanied by General Weygan and saluted the coffin, attended the ceremony on his own initiative.[4] On 12 November 1920 a telegram was sent via the British Ambassador, thanking him for his presence.

The gates and door through which the Unknown Warrior was borne into and out of the chateau at Boulogne. (Author.)

The body being removed from the temporary chapel.
(By kind permission of the Daily Mirror.*)*

Marshal Foch saluting the body on its arrival at the quay.
(By kind permission of the Daily Mirror.*)*

The cortège, which extended over a mile, waited until 10.30 a.m. and on the half hour all the bells of Boulogne rang out as one. At 10.45 a.m. the procession moved off to the sound of Chopin's 'Funeral March'. The fire service led the parade, followed by disabled French soldiers wearing the military medals awarded to them for their war service; next came children of the town, local dignitaries, and then ranks of the French infantry and cavalry. Then came the coffin itself, followed by French soldiers carrying wreaths from the French government, army and navy, and from British armed forces serving in France; behind them were Marshal Foch and Lt Gen.

G. MacDonogh, and finally the remaining officers and troops of the French Army. The route along which the procession passed was lined with French troops and decorated by venetian masts draped with French and British flags. French schoolchildren had been given a holiday, and a crowd of thousands flocked to witness the event. The procession organised by the French authorities could not have been more imposing.

At the Rue Faidherbe, leading to the Port Margaret, the French army played the 'Last Post'. HMS *Verdun* lay at the Quai Gambetta, having left Portland the previous night. (The original plan had been for her to dock at Berth No 1, Quai Chanzy, but she had been delayed by fog.) The atmosphere was one of sombre respect, as the French quite genuinely said good-bye to an ally. So far the French had been responsible for all the ceremony, although at no time was the coffin carried by any other than British and Dominion troops. Soon, however, the Unknown Warrior was to be in the care of his own countrymen.

A telegram sent to Lord Derby made it clear that once the burial party and distinguished guest reached the pier where HMS *Verdun* lay, only British personnel would be involved in moving and placing the casket on to the ship (see Annex A). At the initial planning stage the possibility was discussed of a detachment of French

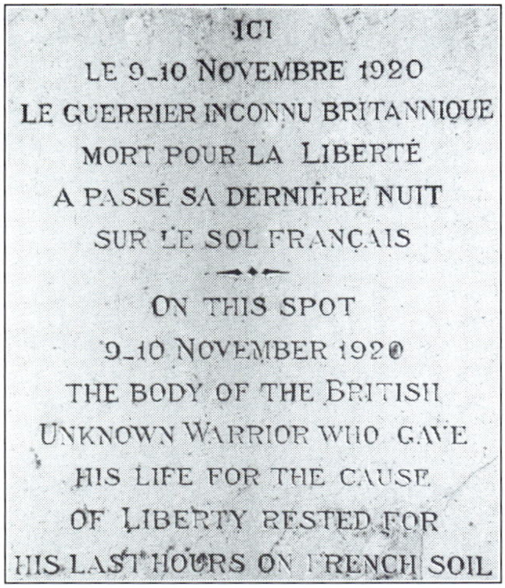

Memorial marking the spot where the Unknown Warrior 'rested for his last hours on French soil'. (Author.)

Marshal Foch and Lt. Gen. George MacDonogh saluting the coffin. (By kind permission of the Daily Mirror.*)*

The coffin and escort. (From The Illustrated London News.*)*

soldiers being allowed to accompany the body to the port of disembarkation (PWo W032/3000 4 Nov 1920) but a meeting of the Army Council decided against this on 6 November, and the final arrangements were sanctioned by the King.[5] The bearer party which had marched beside the horse-drawn wagon since leaving the chateau would be responsible for placing the body on board.

At the pier, both Lt Gen. MacDonogh and Marshal Foch delivered speeches. Marshal Foch saluted and, with a voice full of emotion, said, 'I express the profound feelings of France for the invincible heroism of the British Army, and I regard the body of this hero as a souvenir of the future and as a reminder to work in common to cement the victories we have gained by Eternal Union.' Lt Gen. Sir George MacDonogh stepped forward and, speaking in French, thanked the Marshal on behalf of the King and British government. The band played the national anthems of both countries, then Lt Gen. MacDonogh received the body on behalf of the British nation. On the deck of HMS *Verdun* stood Lt Commander C. S. Thompson and his officers, all wearing No 5 dress, with the Marines dressed in No 2s and carrying rifles with fixed bayonets. The ship's flag flew at half mast and on the quarter deck could be seen the ship's motto *On ne passe pas* (They shall not pass) from the battle cry given by Marshal Pétain to the French Army at the Battle of Verdun in 1916. HMS *Verdun* was named in honour of that battle.[6]

The parade moving down the Rue Faidherbe.
(By kind permission of the Daily Mirror.*)*

The Rue Faidherbe as it is today. (Author.)

Boulogne harbour as it is today. (Author.)

The coffin on board HMS Verdun *prior to departing for Dover.*
(By kind permission of the Daily Mirror.

French artilleryman holding a massive wreath. (By kind permission of the Daily Mirror.*)*

The eight soldiers carried the coffin on to the destroyer and laid it on the bier in the pre-arranged place. They were followed on board by British soldiers carrying wreaths, some so big that four soldiers were required to lift them, and problems were to occur in trying to place these wreaths in the railway luggage van at Dover. Also taken on board were the six barrels of earth taken from the area of Flanders, to be used in the burial.

The naval guard of honour of four blue-jackets of HMS *Verdun* moved into position, Lt Gen. MacDonogh took his place facing the Unknown Warrior at 11.45 and, to the strains of *God Save the King* and the boom of a nineteen-gun salute, HMS *Verdun* slowly moved out and made course for home. Throughout the voyage a naval escort—a single sentry—guarded the precious cargo. Six British destroyers of the Third Flotilla, the Atlantic Fleet waited mid-channel to meet HMS *Verdun* and escort her into Dover harbour. Through the gloom of the dark November day the signal lights of HMS *Verdun* shone out, informing other ships that she and her escort were on their way.

NOTES

1. Much of this chapter has been taken from newspaper accounts, and from other available information.
2. See *Our Empire*, Vol VII, No 8, 1931.
3. *The Daily Telegraph.*
4. PRO WO32/3000.
5. PRO W032/3000, 6 November 1920.
6. See PRO W032/3000, 6 November 1920, paragraph 5: 'A large Union Jack is to be taken to cover the coffin from Boulogne to London.' See Annex A, No. 2

A single sentry guards the body of the Unknown Warrior on board HMS Verdun.
(By kind permission of the Daily Mirror.*)*

4

Home Again (Dover–London)

THE six destroyers awaiting the arrival of HMS *Verdun* were as follows:

HMS *Witherington*	Commander E M W Lawrie
HMS *Wanderer*	Lt Commander B W Owen
HMS *Whitshed*	Lt Commander H A Binmore
HMS *Wivern*	Lt Commander R G H Izat
HMS *Wolverine*	Lt Commander J M Porter
HMS *Veteran*	Commander P G Woodhouse

The ships lowered their Union Flags and ensigns to half mast as the HMS *Verdun* approached. This was a rare honour indeed; an honour which is usually reserved only for the King or the King's representative. The flotilla was due into Dover Harbour at about 3.30 p.m. and, having made the short crossing in good time, HMS *Verdun* laid off Dover by 1.00 p.m. in a cloudy and mist-covered channel. A group of newspaper reporters was taken out to HMS *Verdun* by HMS *Vendetta* to cover the event. HMS *Vendetta*, having lowered her colours also, flashed the signal 'Who are you?', and received in reply the memorable words '*Verdun* and escort, with Unknown Warrior'.

Every vantage point was taken by onlookers. The Prince of Wales Pier was full to overflowing, as were the other piers, and it seemed that everybody in the town and surrounding area had come to pay their respects. Most of the town's shops had closed for the event, and flags were flown at half mast. At 3.15 p.m. the six destroyers of the fleet came into view.[1] As the destroyers headed for the Eastern Dock entrance they parted, and out of the mist came HMS *Verdun*, slowly and gracefully steaming into No 3 berth, Admiralty Pier. A nineteen-gun salute fired by No 11 Battery, Fire Command, Royal Garrison Artillery, sounded as she entered the dock, and the Castle flag was lowered to half mast; an honour only usually accorded to field marshals. Men wept as the military bands struck up 'Land of Hope and Glory'. Rather strangely, the Selection Committee had decided that no ceremony was to be held here on the scale of that in Bolougne, and only a small reception party waited on the pier.

The route to Berth No 3 was lined by troops of the 2nd Battalion Royal Irish Fusiliers in Guard of Honour order, with Colour and Regimental Bands on parade. The crew of HMS *Verdun* were assembled, and four blue-jackets, heads bowed and rifles reversed, stood at each corner of the casket, which

Dover harbour entrance today.
(Author.)

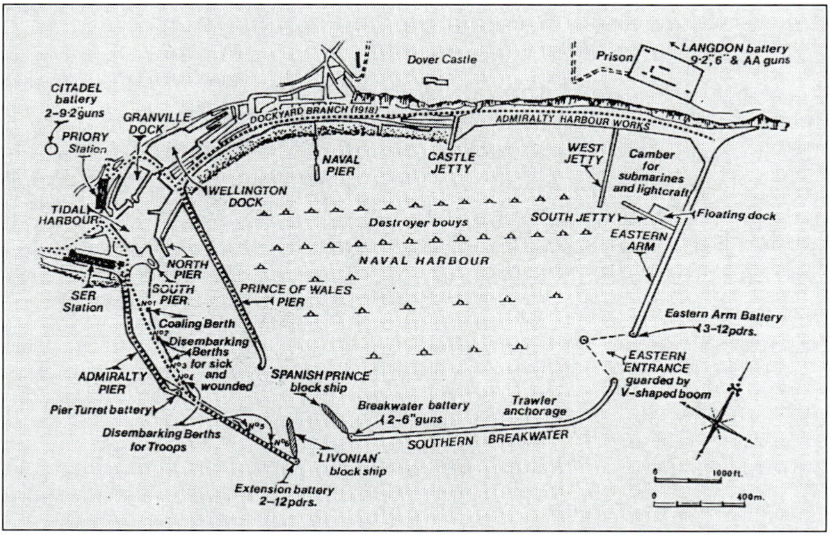

Plan of Dover harbour in 1918.
(Dover Museum.)

HMS Verdun *entering Dover harbour.*
(By kind permission of The Illustrated London News.*)*

HMS Verdun *docking at Dover.*
(By kind permission of The Illustrated London News.*)*

The coffin being carried off HMS Verdun *at Dover.*
(By kind permission of the Daily Mirror.*)*

could not itself be seen as it was covered with the giant wreaths which had been laid upon it at Bolougne. Lt Gen. MacDonogh had again taken up his place at the head of the coffin. Six bearers boarded the ship, all warrant officers, from the Royal Navy, No 11 Fire Command Royal Garrison Artillery, 2nd Bn Royal Irish Fusiliers, 2nd Bn Connaught Rangers, Royal Marines and Royal Air Force. As the coffin was borne down the gang-plank HMS *Verdun* sounded the 'Still', Colours were lowered, the Regimental Band of the Irish Fusiliers struck up the 'General Salute', and every sailor paid his respects. It was with this wonderful vigilant silence that Dover received the Unknown Warrior back on to English soil.

The coffin was received by General Sir J. Longley, commanding the Eastern Area, and Colonel Knight, Commander Dover Garrison. The pall bearers, lieutenant colonels or equivalent rank from the Navy, Marines, Army and Air Force, were: Commander Norfolk, OC Royal Marines; Colonel R. B. Riddell DSO RGA; Colonel R. G. Shuter DSO, 2nd Bn Royal Irish Fusiliers and the OC RAF.

Immediately after the King's representative came Maj. Gen. Sir J. R. Longley and Colonel Knight, then officers from the Dover Corporation headed by the Town Sergeant with the mace and followed by the Mayor and members of the Council, all dressed in their gowns. The minutes clerk had

The coffin being carried along Admiralty Pier.
(By kind permission of the Dover Express.*)*

The pier today.
(Author.)

Dover Marine Station.
(Author.)

earlier placed a wreath on the coffin on behalf of the town. Also in the procession were off-duty officers of the Dover Garrison.[2]

The coffin was borne along, passing the one hundred soldiers from the Connaught Rangers, fifty from the 2nd Bn Royal West Kent Regiment, and representatives of Dover Garrison. To the tune of 'Scipio' the party made its way to the western platform of the Marine Station, from which the train was due to leave at 5.50 p.m.[3] Here, formed up into a square, stood the Guard of Honour of the 2nd Bn Connaught Rangers consisting of three officers and a hundred other ranks with Colour and Regimental Band, and pupils from the Duke of York's Royal Military School, their uniforms adding colour to the occasion.[4]

The coffin was to be placed in passenger luggage van No 132 of the South Eastern and Chatham Railway Company; the same van which had carried both Nurse Edith Cavell and Captain Charles Fryatt. The story of Nurse Cavell is well documented, but the story of Captain Charles Fryatt is not as well known. While commanding the Great Eastern Railway steamer *Brussels* on its regular run between the Hook of Holland and Harwich, he had rammed a German submarine. This exploit won him much praise and he was presented with an engraved cigarette case in commemoration of the event. Less than two months later his ship was intercepted by the Germans and Captain

Luggage van, S. E. and Chatham Railway 132.
(Author.)

Fryatt and his crew were taken to a POW Camp outside Berlin where he was accused of piracy. He was executed on 27 July 1916 in Bruges.

As the coffin reached the carriage, the Connaught Rangers presented arms and the 'General Salute' was given. The bearer party slowly entered the luggage van and placed the oak casket on the raised bier which had been fitted by the railway men of the South Eastern and Chatham Railway Co. in London a few days earlier. The roof of the van containing the casket had been painted white so that it could easily be identified by the crowds waiting along the route, the van interior walls had been draped in

Topaz train engine No. 737.
(This is not the actual train used).
(Author.)

The guard over the coffin at Dover station.
(By kind permission of the Daily Mirror.*)*

purple, and a lattice of bay, chrysanthemums and rosemary formed a frieze around the compartment. The bearer party and the Guard of Honour of the Duke of York's Military School then marched off and four sentries, selected from the troops of the Dover Garrison, were placed outside the van to stand guard over the casket until the train moved off. What could be seen were the huge wreaths that had, with difficulty, been placed in the van, some requiring four to five men to move them. Over an hour remained before the train was due to depart, and only a select few were allowed near the van. Some of the more enterprising simply bought train tickets to gain entrance to the station.

Very few of the waiting crowd were able to witness much of the ceremony at all. There was very little room, everything was over quickly, and there was no time at all for the people of Dover to pay their respects. This was a source of grievance for some time after, for Dover, like elsewhere, had lost loved ones, and had been one of the main casualty clearing station during the war; between 1915 and 1918, 3,166 hospital ships had berthed and 7,515 ambulance trains with 1,215,886 wounded on board had departed from the station. Nevertheless, they stood there in dense masses about the station and harbour to honour the unknown hero.

The van containing the casket and wreaths, and another for the guard consisting of one officer and fifteen NCOs and privates of the Connaught Rangers, had been attached to the 5.50 p.m. boat train from Dover to London Victoria, travelling via Canterbury. The Guard of Honour of the 2nd Bn Connaught Rangers took up their position at 5.20 p.m. and presented arms, the band again played the 'General Salute' as the Colours were lowered, and the train which bore the Unknown Warrior pulled away. At the 'up'

Victoria Station, platform 8.
(Author.)

platform of Harbour Station the Guard of Honour of the Royal Irish Fusiliers presented arms.

The train moved through the Kent countryside, making its way towards London. Did the warrior know this area? Had he been a boy here? Or had he, like millions of other British Tommies, simply passed this way, on his way to the embarkation docks at Dover and Folkestone, for his journey to the Western Front? The *Daily Mirror* reported the warrior's journey as follows.

The train stations en route were filled to overflowing, with every vantage point taken. At Faversham ex-servicemen crowded the platform, carrying the union flag surmounted by a wreath of bay leaves, while the 'Last Post' was played by a detachment of boy scouts. Blue-jackets formed the guard of honour at Gillingham station, resting with bowed heads on their reversed rifles. At Chatham the military tribute was paid by the Royal Warwickshire Regiment, who presented arms as the train departed. When the train did stop at stations along the route, a detachment of the escort stood guard over the carriage.

As the train approached Victoria Station, crowds which had been gathering since early evening saw the carriage for the first time. There was for a while a panic as thousands threatened to push aside the temporary barriers and the small number of police present. Some attempted to climb on to the engine and carriage.

The carriage carrying the body and the other van were detached from the train at Victoria Station and moved on to the London Brighton and South Coast line from the South Eastern and Chatham, a special brake having been installed to assist this operation.

At 8.32 p.m., having taken thirty minutes to change track and be shunted into place, it pulled in to the area of platform 8 at the station's Buckingham Palace Road entrance. The waiting reception party consisted of Lt Gen. Sir George MacDonogh who had accompanied the body from France, his aide, Capt. Lyon and Maj. Warner DSO MC Brigade Major of the Brigade of Guards. All saluted as the carriage came to a halt. The King's Company the 1st Bn Grenadier Guards supplied the guard at the station, presenting arms as the train drew in. The guard consisted of one officer, Lt Gregson-Ellis (who was handed the key to the padlocked van), sixteen NCOs and guardsmen.[5] The Connaught Rangers who had accompanied the van exchanged military salutes with the new guard and marched away, their task completed.

The carriage remained closed and attached to the saloon, while the saloon was to be used as a temporary guard room for the night. Wreaths still covered the casket, and the luggage van stood in darkness, screened from prying eyes. The wreaths were taken to the Jerusalem Chamber at the Abbey ready for the ceremony the next day.

Outside the station a large crowd had gathered, standing in silence, some sobbing, paying their respects to a fallen comrade—the term which Railton preferred to 'Warrior'.[6] In the background the noise of trains could still be heard while the silent ranks strained to catch a glimpse of the carriage. Eventually they all drifted away, leaving a silence which seemed to linger. Two guardsmen remained, arms reversed and heads bowed, one at each side of the luggage van door, beginning their night vigil. For the next day was to see the most remarkable military funeral ever witnessed by the citizens of the empire's capital city.

NOTES

1. Three destroyers were in line abreast, forward of HMS *Verdun* which was alone. The remaining three were abreast astern. HMS *Verdun* had a white band painted around its funnel to distinguish it from the rest—the sign of a ship from the fourth flotilla.
2. See PRO WO32/3000 for the instructions covering the ceremony for the receiving of the body and its dispatch to London. 9, 10 November 1920.

3.. Dover Marine Station was built in 1899 by SECR, an amalgamation of the SER and LCDR railway companies. SER's London route was via Folkestone, LCDR's was via Canterbury, and both routes are still in service today. The station finally entered commercial service on 18 January 1919, having been commandeered as a military station in 1914. It did not open fully until 1916.

4. Much of the above has been extracted from the newspapers of the time which, it should be remembered, played a leading role in reporting and covering the event. They were after all the only means available to the public for news, indeed both the *Daily Mirror* and *The Times* were to bring out souvenir supplements covering the burial on 11 November, price at one penny for the twenty-page edition

5. The rank of Guardsman was granted by King George V in 1919.

6. See *Our Empire*, Vol VII, No. 8, 1931: 'The only request the Noble Dean did not see his way to granting was the suggestion I gave him—from a relative of mine—that the tomb should be described as that of the Unknown "Comrade" rather than "Warrior" . . .'

WESTMINSTER ABBEY.

✝

THE FUNERAL SERVICE

OF

A British Warrior

ON

THE SECOND ANNIVERSARY

OF THE SIGNING OF

THE ARMISTICE.

NOVEMBER 11th, 1920.

Form of Service, 11 November 1920.
(By kind permission of the Dean and Chapter, Westminster.)

5

The Nation Mourns

CROWDS began to assemble early on the morning of Thursday 11 November. It was not long before the best viewing positions along the route were taken, and the area around Victoria Station was soon full, with crowds of six or seven deep on the pavements. In different parts of the station, trains arrived and departed as usual, but on platform 8 the area around the carriage remained cordoned and screened from the eyes of onlookers. The Guardsmen from the King's Company Grenadier Guards maintained their vigil, heads bowed and rifles reversed, having been relieved at thirty-minute intervals during the night.[1] The guards were to remain at their station until the body was removed and placed on the gun carriage for its journey to the Cenotaph and finally to rest at Westminster Abbey.

Areas of Whitehall had been set aside for members of the royal family, parliament and representatives from the Dominions, the three armed services, as well as war widows and members of the ex-services associations. The general public were advised where they should stand for the procession, as the numbers were expected to be in the hundreds of thousands. The *Daily Mirror* published the route and times for the procession, as follows:

Victoria Station	9.40	The Mall	10.20
Grosvenor Place	9.45	Admiralty Arch	10.30
Hyde Park Corner	10.00	Whitehall	10.35
Wellington Arch	10.05	Parliament Street	10.45
Constitution Hill	10.10		

> At quarter past eight on this morning, the doors of the barricades at Trafalgar Square, Bridge Street and Tothill Street, Whitehall will be opened to admit a limited number of the public.

The responsibility for the smooth running of this historic event rested upon a staff officer.

Shortly after 8.00 a.m. troops and ex-servicemen began to arrive—828 all ranks in total, from all three services. The troops formed up into three ranks and the ex-servicemen (all with medals and some in military uniform) into four ranks. At 9.15 a.m. the firing party, gun carriage and bearers[2] were waiting in position on platform 8 at Victoria Station. The massed bands of the Guards Division had taken up their places at the station entrance by

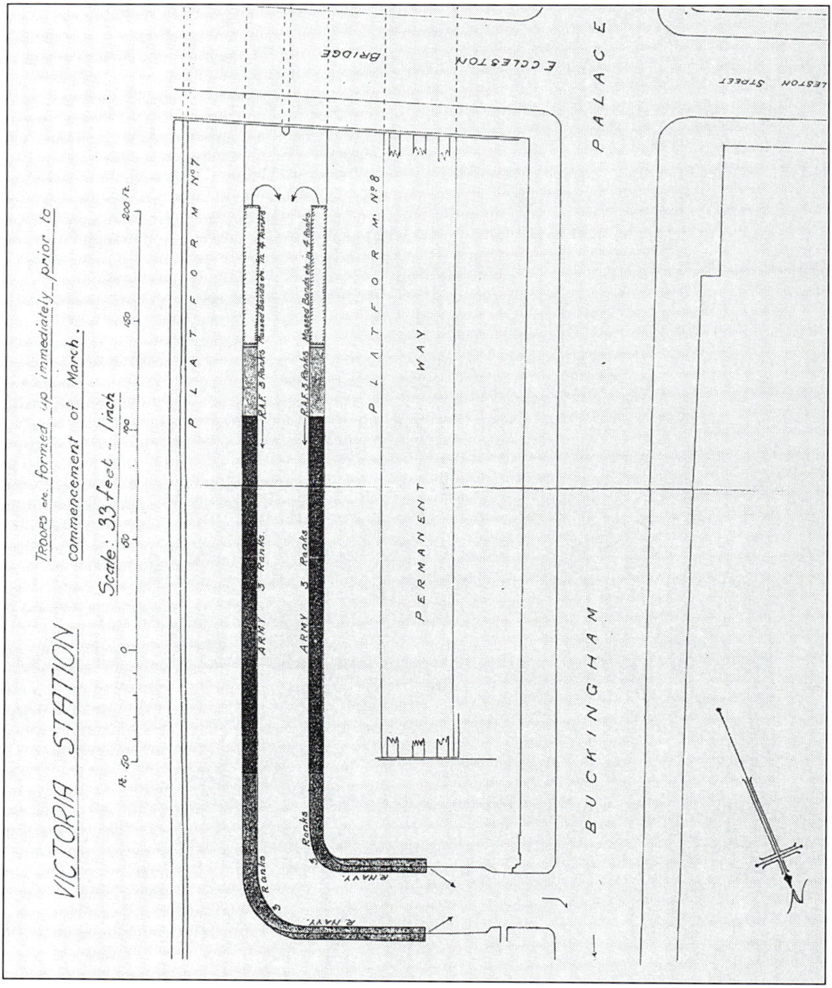
VICTORIA STATION
TROOPS etc. formed up immediately prior to commencement of March.
Scale: 33 feet - 1 inch
PLATFORM No 7
PLATFORM No 8
PERMANENT WAY
ARMY 3 Ranks
R.A.F. 3 Ranks
Massed Bands etc. in 4 Ranks
R. NAVY.
ECCLESTON BRIDGE
BUCKINGHAM PALACE

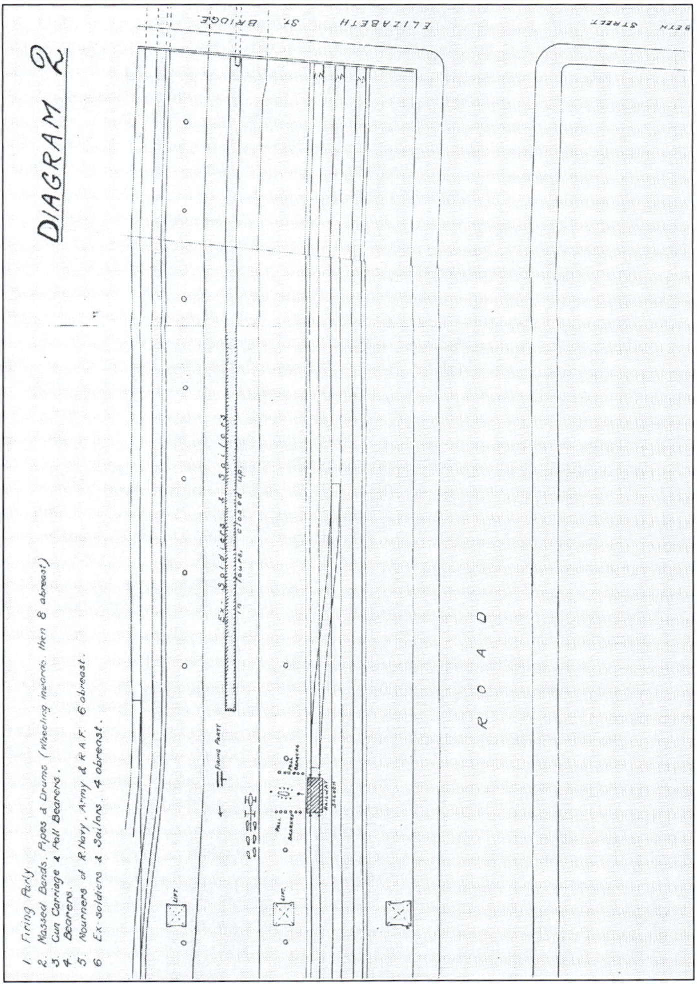

Diagrams showing the formation of the cortège at Victoria Station. (By kind permission of the Public Record Office.)

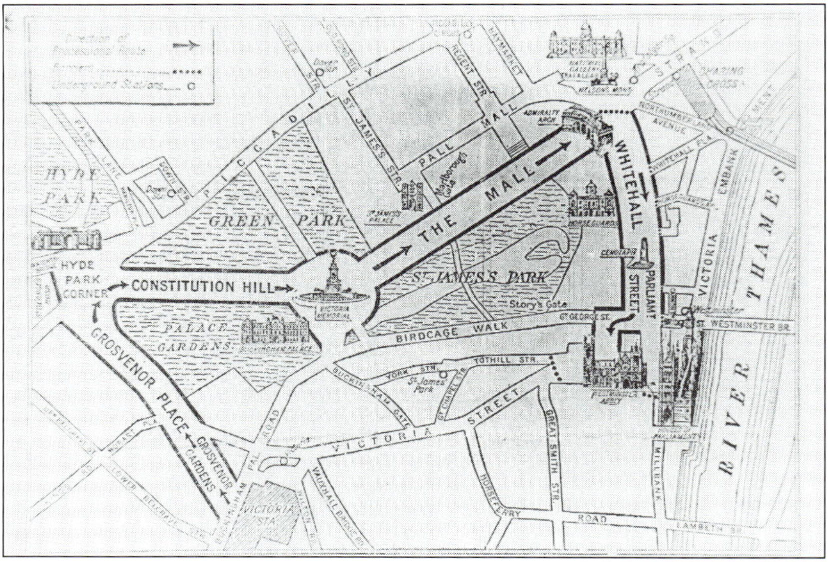

Above: Map showing the route to be taken. (By kind permission of The Daily Telegraph.*)*
Below: Archway through which the cortège left Victoria Station. (Author.)

9.18, the Royal Air Force by 9.20, the Army by 9.23 and finally the Royal Navy at 9.25 (see diagram).

Outside the station, and on the route to the Cenotaph and Westminster Abbey, every vantage point was now taken, the crowds now numbering in the tens of thousands. Everywhere there was a strange silence, apart from the sobs of those for whom the strain proved too much, and the children in the crowd stood quiet and subdued. But no-one present wanted to miss the occasion: they had come to pay their homage.

Not only was London swamped by a mass of people but, as the hour of 11 a.m. drew near, crowds began to assemble in every city, town and village across the nation. They, too, were waiting to pay their respects. In London alone,

The Mall. (Author.)

thirty-five thousand soldiers and policemen were required for duty.

The funeral coach had now been drawn from its position and was placed alongside platform 8, and the six barrels containing the soil from France had already been sent to Westminster to be used to cover the coffin once it had been lowered into the prepared grave.

At 9.20 a.m. the bearer party of eight guardsmen of the 3rd Bn Coldstream Guards,[3] commanded by a sergeant, entered the luggage van that contained the great oak coffin of the Unknown Warrior. On the coffin they placed a Union Flag, steel helmet and side arms of a private soldier of the British Army, which they made secure on the torn battle flag which covered it. The *Daily Telegraph* reporter covering the event wrote as follows:

> Then a sharp command, and simultaneously everyone was presenting arms. In that one moment I realised more than words can tell, the tremendous significance of that very simple coffin . . .

Raising the coffin onto their shoulders, they carried it the short distance to the waiting gun-carriage, which was drawn up opposite the railway's saloon, facing Eccleston Bridge. The coffin was lowered and secured, and the bearer party stepped back and marched to their position at the rear of the gun-carriage.[4] As the coffin was laid on the gun carriage there came from Hyde

Admiralty Arch. (Author.)

Park the sounds of artillery fire as N Battery (St John's Wood) Royal Horse Artillery began the nineteen-gun salute.

The procession now waited in the bright November sun. Ahead lay 3,960 yards of road between Victoria Station and the Cenotaph, and, finally, the Abbey. The firing party, presenting arms, moved to their position at the head of the massed bands of the Household Division, the twelve distinguished pall bearers saluted and then placed themselves at either side of the gun carriage. There they stood, the nation's highest ranking officers: Admiral of the Fleet, The Hon. Sir Hedworth Meux; Admiral of the Fleet, Earl Beatty; Admiral of the Fleet, Sir Henry Jackson; General Albert Farrar Gatliff, Royal Marines; Admiral Sir Charles Madden; Field Marshal Sir Henry Wilson; Field Marshal Lord Methuen; Field Marshal Viscount French; Field Marshal Earl Haig; General Lord Byng; General Lord Horne, and Air Marshal Hugh Trenchard Bt. Field Marshal Sir W. Robertson and Admiral Sir F. C. Doveton were both unable to take part.

At 9.40 the parade moved off in slow time to Chopin's 'Funeral March' and to the sound of drums muffled with black cloth. At the same time four mounted policemen moved out from Victoria Station, making sure the route was clear. Six black horses pulled the gun carriage, preceded by the massed bands and flanked by the twelve military commanders. Then came the

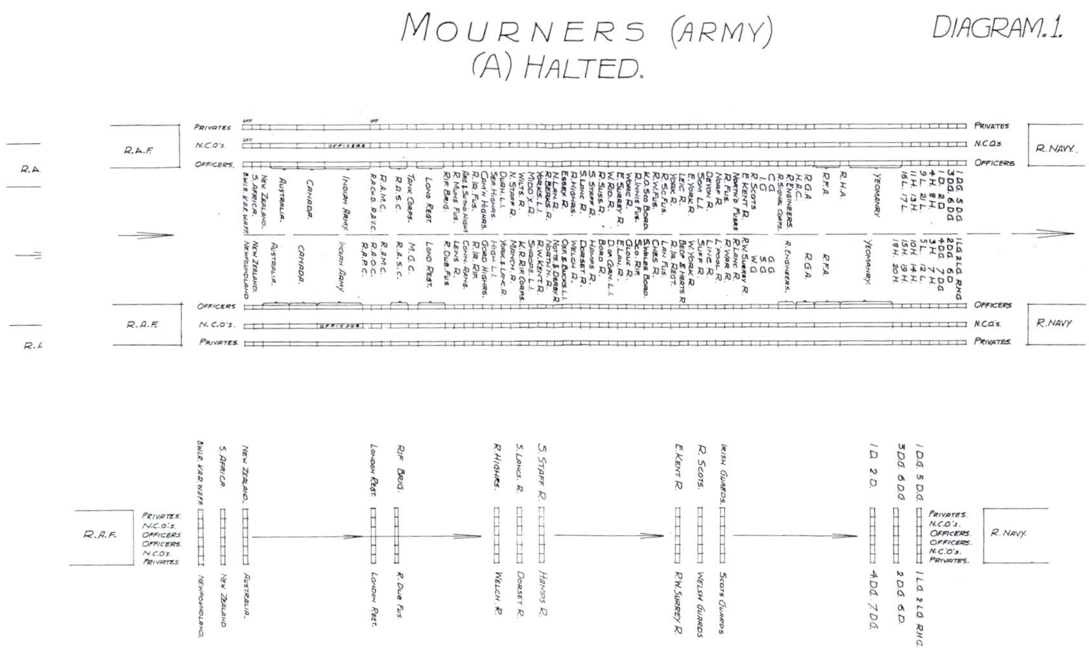

Mourners halted (A) and on the march (B). By kind permission of the Public Record Office.

His Majesty King George V, the nation's chief mourner.
By kind permission of The Illustrated London News.

The gun-carriage at the Cenotaph.
(By kind permission of the Imperial War Museum.)

mourners of the armed services, next four hundred ex-servicemen who, without regard to rank or service, marched four abreast, following their comrade-in-arms.

The people in the area of Hyde Park could now hear, in the distance, the pipers of the Scots Guards playing the lament 'Flowers of the Forest', while through the crowd of over fifty thousand assembled in Trafalgar Square a whisper began to convey the message: 'He's coming'. Then came the music and the gun carriage. It was an emotional appeal which was at once answered, for the crowd sobbed in genuine grief. The lasting impressions of the day were the silence, and the image of the gun carriage with the coffin placed high upon it, covered by the battle flag, ripped and torn, its colours standing out on this bright day. Englishmen and women sobbed and were not ashamed.

As the procession reached each detachment of soldiers lining the route, the soldiers reversed arms and lowered their heads. The men in the crowd bared their heads in silent respect. For those who remembered the war and had lost friends, this was a chance to say a final farewell. Slowly marching to the sound of the bass drums, the cortège moved on, along Grosvenor Gardens and Grosvenor Place, making a sharp turn towards Constitution Hill, then into the Mall and through the centre gates of Admiralty Arch into Trafalgar Square.

His Majesty King George V pressing the button to unveil the Cenotaph. (By kind permission of the Daily Mirror.*)*

At 10.40 the King, dressed in the uniform of a Field Marshal, took up his position facing the Cenotaph, which was still covered by two huge union flags. A pace to his rear stood his sons also in military uniforms. The prime minister, members of all political parties, foreign dignitaries, ex-servicemen and war widows all stood in silence as the procession made its way to the east of the Cenotaph and the gun-carriage came to rest in front of the King (see diagram page 57). The King saluted and stepping forward, placed on the coffin a wreath of red roses and bay leaves with the inscription, written in his own hand:

In proud memory of those warriors who died unknown in the Great War.
Unknown, and yet well known, as dying and behold they lived.
George R I.

The band played 'O God Our Help in Ages Past', only the choir, it seemed, singing. At the end of the hymn the Archbishop of Canterbury rose and, after a pause, began the Lord's Prayer, the choir repeating it with him. Then came silence as the crowd waited for the chimes of Big Ben to sound. At 11 o'clock Big Ben struck, and on the last note the King pressed the button which released first the Union Flag on the southern side of the Cenotaph and

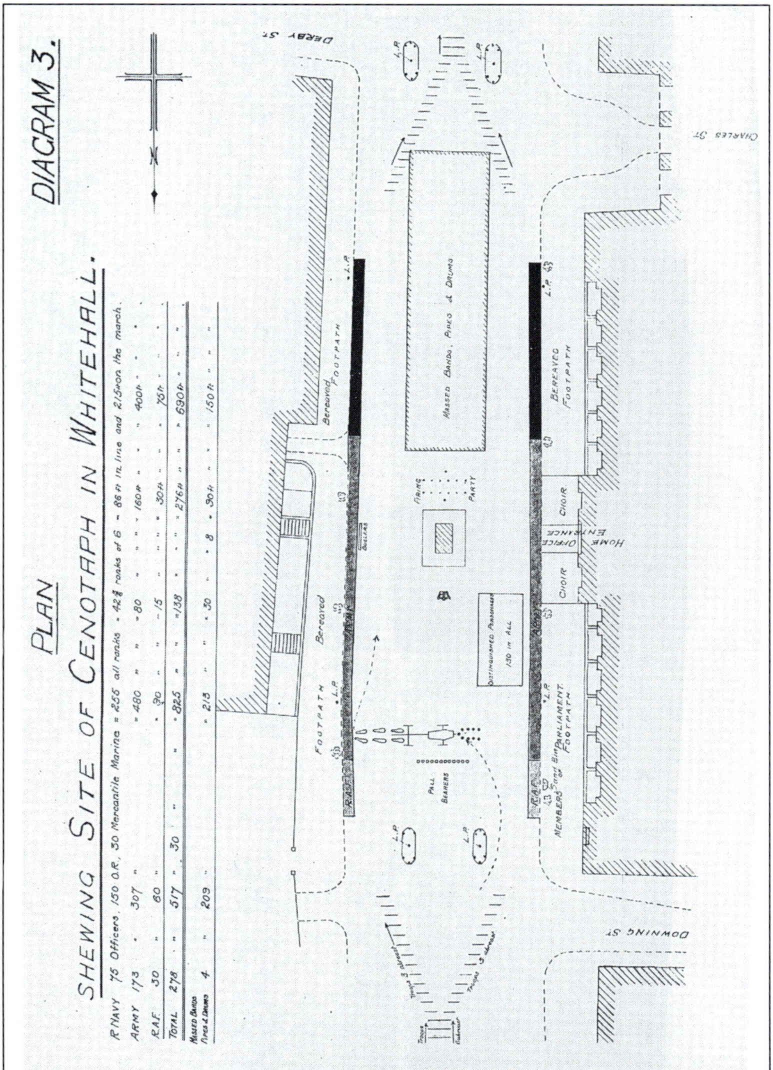

Plan showing the site of the Cenotaph in Whitehall. (By kind permission of the Public Record Office.)

Silence.
(By kind permission of the Daily Mirror.*)*

then that on the northern side, so that the austere grey mass was exposed for all to see—an everlasting reminder, to all who pass by, of British valour. The two minute silence began.

The whole nation remembered the dead of the Great War, as the two-minute silence was observed in cities, towns and villages throughout the country, even though some towns and cities had no officially organised Remembrance Service. An excellent example is given in the *Manchester Evening News* (11 November 1920, p. 4) in a story headed 'Silent Cells':[5]

> A case which was part heard was suspended, the accused—an ex-soldier who has served in France, Eqypt and Mesopotamia and gained the DCM and the Croix de Guerre—springing smartly to attention between the warders standing on either side of him. The recorder . . . Counsel, solicitors, prison officers and members of the Police all paid silent tribute. Prisoners in the cells, some of them awaiting removal to Strangeways Gaol to serve sentences, rigidly observed the silence.

Across the capital, from St Paul's to the Roman Catholic Cathedral at Victoria, the city came to a halt. Men and women wept openly. At the Mansion House, Royal Exchange and the Bank of England, Union Flags flew at half mast, as they did across the country.

His Majesty the King laying the first tribute. (By kind permission of the Daily Mirror.*)*

Her Majesty the Queen entering the Abbey.
(By kind permission of The Illustrated London News.*)*

His Majesty King George V following the coffin down Whitehall.
(By kind permission of The Illustrated London News.*)*

Parliament Square.
(By kind permission of The Illustrated London News.*)*

At the end of the two minutes' silence the King took from an officer in the army a wreath which he placed on the northern face of the Cenotaph. This time the flowers were white, and the inscription read as follows:

Buckingham Palace
In memory of the glorious dead
from George R I and Mary R, November the 11th, 1920

Words of command rang out sharply, the firing-party wheeled into place, the bands fell in and the pall bearers placed themselves at either side of the coffin, behind which came the King as the nation's and Empire's chief mourner. Next were Prince of Wales and his brothers followed by the Prime Minister, the Speaker and representatives from the armed services, all of whom had laid wreaths at the Cenotaph. Headed by the Guards' bands and followed by the Bishop of London and the Archbishop of Canterbury, the column moved down Whitehall to the Abbey, once again to the music of Chopin's 'Funeral March'.

At the Cenotaph, barriers were quickly put in place and four sentries were posted, one at each corner of the Cenotaph: on the north-eastern corner Royal Navy; north-western Royal Marines; south-western Army; south-eastern RAF. Then seemingly endless columns of people, led by men

Coldstream Guards lowering the coffin into the grave.
(By kind permission of The Illustrated London News.*)*

His Majesty the King scattering soil over the coffin.
(By kind permission of The Illustrated London News.*)*

in wheelchairs and dressed in hospital blue, thronged towards to the nation's new memorial: Chelsea pensioners, war widows, representatives from ex-servicemen associations, veterans all. For the rest of the day the pile of flowers grew as wreaths of all shapes and sizes, handfuls of flowers, a single rose, were placed on the memorial. Most florists in the capital had sold out by the end of the day, and the base of the Cenotaph soon disappeared under the weight of lilies, roses and laurels.[6] Over one hundred thousand wreaths were to be placed at the Cenotaph by the end of five days.[7] The nation was indeed paying its respects. So the people came on and on, as if all the nation was to pass by.

At the Abbey, where the Band of the Grenadier Guards had been playing whilst the ceremony at the Cenotaph was in progress, the Queen was waiting accompanied by the Queen of Spain, the Queen of Norway and the ladies of the royal household. (The Queen had made her way by car to the Abbey after watching the ceremony at the Cenotaph.) The Abbey itself was filled by nearly one thousand widows and mothers of those who had fallen in the Great War. Outside a large crowd remained silent.

As the procession halted at the Abbey gates the music ceased. The bearer party of the Coldstream Guards, having placed their rifles on the grass near the wall of the Abbey, moved into position. In the deep silence which had

One hundred holders of the Victoria Cross paying their last respects.
(By kind permission of The Illustrated London News.*)*

covered the whole of Parliament Square, these tall guardsmen raised their comrade and, with the King saluting, made their way into the Abbey. Never had any hero of the nation had so distinguished a ceremony.[8] Passing between lines of Empire soldiers, the coffin was carried feet first through the north transept door, where it was met by the Dean, Chapter and clergy of the Abbey. Still borne on the shoulders of the guardsmen, the coffin was slow marched with impeccable precision between two lines made up of the one hundred holders of the Victoria Cross, the nation's highest award for bravery.[9] This unique guard of honour was commanded by Colonel Freyberg VC, Grenadier Guards.

'I am the Resurrection and the Life', written by Croft and Purcell, was sung as the procession made its way from the north porch to the centre of the nave, where the grave had been prepared.[10] People strained to see the coffin as it passed, and sobs could be heard as the Dean began to conduct the service for the Burial of the Dead. The King took up his place at the head of the grave, facing west, with the royal princes behind him. At the foot of the grave stood the Dean with the Archbishop of Canterbury, the Bishop of London and other church dignitaries. On either side of the grave were the distinguished pall bearers, soldiers facing north, airmen and sailors facing south, while east of the grave stood rows of ministers with Mr Lloyd George and Mr Asquith both in the front row. Close by was the choir, placed in a semi-circle near to the grave.

'Equale for Trombones' by Beethoven was now played, the Twenty-third Psalm, 'The Lord is My Shepherd', was sung, and the Dean read the lesson, taken from the seventh chapter of the Book of Revelations. As the hymn 'Lead Kindly Light' was begun the bearer party stepped forward to lower the coffin into the grave. Mr Wright, clerk of works to the Abbey, placed in the hands of Sir Douglas Dawson a silver shell filled with earth taken from the battlefields of Flanders. Sir Douglas in turn handed the shell to the King who sprinkled the earth over the coffin as the Dean said, 'Earth to earth, ashes to ashes'. The grave was to be partly filled with the Flanders soil which had travelled with the coffin, making a part of the Abbey forever a foreign field. The service ended with Kipling's 'Recessional' and the blessing. The silence which followed was broken by the 'Last Post' and 'Reveille' from the drums and trumpets of the musicians ranged on the steps west of King Henry VII Chapel. As the Grenadier Guards played the 'Grand Solemn March' by G. J. Miller, the King, Dean, clergy and the distinguished party of civil and military dignitaries left the Abbey by the west door.

Immediately after the service the grave was covered with the 'Actors' Pall'[11] and the union flag, and four sentries were mounted: Royal Navy to the south east; Royal Marines north east; Army north west, and Royal Air

Crowds passing the grave.
(By kind permission of the Daily Mirror.*)*

The crowd makes its way to the nation's monument.
(By kind permission of the Daily Mirror.*)*

Police were kept busy, laying wreaths for thousands of absent mourners.
(By kind permission of the Daily Mirror.*)*

The crowd in Trafalgar Square. (By kind permission of the Daily Mirror.*)*

The tomb today.
(By kind permission of the Dean and Chapter, Westminster.)

Force south west. They were to remain in place until 4.30 p.m., the guard being changed every twenty minutes. Two vans arrived, bringing from HMS *Verdun* the remaining wreaths which had come from France with the body and were now to placed in the Abbey with those sent the previous night. Outside the north door of the Abbey stood a queue, four deep, reaching as far as the Cenotaph. Mr Nicholson, the Abbey organist, and four fellow organists took turns to play during the time that the Abbey was open to the public. (Gramophone records of the service and music could be purchased for 7*s*. 6*d*. each. It is believed these were the first recordings ever made in the Abbey.)[12] By 27 November over one and a half million people had passed the grave.

Lord Stamfordham sent a letter of thanks to the Dean on behalf of the King, informing him that 'His Majesty sincerely thanks you and all concerned for the perfect manner in which everything was carried out',[13] and on his return to Buckingham Palace the King entered this line in his personal diary: 'Got home at 12 o'clock, everything was most beautifully arranged and carried out.'[14]

At the end of the first week the Actors' Pall was removed and the grave sealed and covered with a large slab of Tournai Marble bearing the simple inscription

A British Warrior
who fell
in The Great War
1914–1918
FOR KING
AND COUNTRY
Greater Love Hath No Man
Than This

For those who will visit the Abbey, visit the grave and stand for a while and remember that under that black marble gravestone lies a man who went to do his duty for his God, his king and his country—principles we perhaps do not fully understand today. But when the Abbey doors closed on that November evening seventy-five years ago they closed on a piece of our history which belonged to one man: a man who for two minutes held the thoughts of the nation and the empire and the memories of those who fought and lived through the war which he was to represent.

The last words should perhaps be those of the Reverend David Railton himself:

> No one knows the Unknown Warrior's rank, his wealth, his education or his history. Class values become vanity there.[15]

NOTES

1. The Grenadier Guards were to carry Sir Winston Churchill to his funeral service.
2. N Battery, Royal Horse Artillery supplied both the six black horses and the gun carriage. They were represented in the cortège by Lt. E. M. Tyler MC and Bdr. Gilbert and Gnr. Jones.
3. The Coldstream Guards were, years later, to bury another Field Marshal, Montgomery of El Alamein.

4. For the military-minded, the orders covering the ceremony for 'The Burial in Westminster Abbey of the body of an Unknown British Warrior and the Unveiling of the Cenotaph in Whitehall by His Majesty the King', may I recommend two sources: PWO 30/3000, Public Record Office, Kew; RHQ Coldstream Guards, Birdcage Walk, London who kindly forwarded a copy to the author. All watches were to be synchronised by the hands of Big Ben.
5. By kind permission *Manchester Evening News.*
6. The original Cenotaph, with its flags (see photograph, page 4), was for many years housed at the War Museum at the Crystal Palace. It was the King's wish that as many ex-servicemen should attend the ceremony, wearing medals and decorations. That the 'two minute silence' should be observed by the National and Empire.
7. The *Daily Mirror* organised the laying of wreaths for its readers. *Daily Mirror*, 12 November 1920, p. 5.
8. Railton, in his account written in 1931, mentioned that one of the reasons why he did not trust some of the King's advisers was that he feared that the soldier could end up in some out-of-the-way place, as Lord Kitchener had. See *Our Empire*, Vol VII, No 8, 1931.
9. 634 VCs were awarded during the war. The 100 VCs were selected by lots from 350 holders of the award. The coffin was carried to its appointed place in the Nave, where the Bearer Party placed it on to the wooden bars which covered the grave. See also Cave, Terry, CBE, 'The Unknown Warrior', The Western Front Association's Bulletin No. 17, October 1986, who puts the number at ninety-six men decorated for gallantry.
10. When the grave was dug it was found that no other burial had taken place in that spot in the thousand-year history of the Abbey. The grave was later filled with soil brought from France.
11. The Actors' Pall had been given by that profession to remember their fellow artists who had died in the war, and is still used in the Abbey (see photograph, page 16.)
12. *The Age of Illusion*, pp. 10, 11.
13. RA Geo V 01637/12
14. Extract from King George V's diary.
15. *Our Empire*, Vol VII, No 8, 1931.

Westminster Abbey.
(Author.)

Summary

THAT day in November 1920 was one to remember for those who fought and for those who had lost loved ones. Sadly, in less than twenty years the country and Empire were to be at war again. The number of people who have passed by the grave of the Unknown Warrior since that day seventy-five years ago is incalculable. How many of them understand what it represents today?

On Armistice day 1921, the black marble grave stone which had been made in Belgium replaced the temporary one. On the same day the Reverend David Railton carried his own flag, which had been used the year before, to the altar to be dedicated and placed in the Abbey. It hangs now in St George's Chapel. A month earlier General Pershing placed on the grave the American Congressional Medal of Honour, which can still be seen in the Abbey in a glass-covered box near to the grave. The Victoria Cross was awarded to the American Unknown Soldier.

HMS *Verdun*, the V/W Class Destroyer, was broken up on 3 March 1946 at Ward Inverkeithing. Her ship's bell has hung in the nave of Westminster Abbey since 1990. The bell is rung at midday every day (except Sunday) to remember the dead of all wars.

The carriage that bore the casket and Luggage Van 132 of the former South Eastern and Chatham Railway, can still be seen (with white-painted roof) at the time of writing at Robertsbridge, East Sussex. The locomotive used on the day has since been scrapped, but an engine of the same class is on display at the National Railway Museum, York, Locomotive Number 737.

King George V died on 20 January 1936.

The Reverend David Railton, MA MC, died in an accident in his beloved Scotland in 1955, falling from a train as it approached Fort William, Inverness-shire.

Brigadier General Wyatt died 25 April 1955.

The Rt Rev. Herbert Ryle died in 1925 and is buried in the nave at Westminster Abbey. It was he who supplied the inscription on the black marble grave stone.

It is still possible to see many of the places used on that November day and follow the route taken: very little has changed, in London at least. The docks at Dover have changed greatly over the years, with, for example, the Hoverport.

Lt General Sir George MacDonogh died on 10 July 1942.

Marshal Foch died in Paris in 1929.

Sir Douglas Dawson died on 20 January 1936.

Lord Curzon died on 20 March 1925.

Rudyard Kipling died on 18 January 1936.

The Australian Unknown Warrior was buried on 11 November 1993 at the Australian Monument, Canberra.

The Admiralty Pier and Dover Marine Station still stand, but the station closed in September 1994. Arrangements have to be made to visit the pier where the body was landed with Stena Sealink who are very helpful.

Admission to the Abbey on 11 November was by ticket only. Instructions had been given by the Memorial Services Sub-Committee. The arrangements were as follows:

1. That one ticket admits one person only.
2. That tickets for Westminster Abbey and for standing . . .
3. The tickets for windows in Government offices are for women only . . .
4. That only one ticket has been issued to one family . . .
5. That persons who applied for tickets . . .
6. That as soon as possible enclosures in letters of application will be returned to the sender.

The Daily Telegraph, November 1920.

Platform 8 at Victoria Station is still there but much of the surrounding area of the station has changed. It is still possible to see the different stations which were in existence in the 1920s, to leave the station by the same arched doorway as was used on that day and to walk by the same route to Westminster Abbey.

The French selected their Unknown Warrior from eight battlefields. Nine battlefields were first chosen, but at the ninth there were no remains which could be regarded for certain as being those of a French solider. The eight coffins were sent to the Citadel of Verdun and remained in state. In the presence of M. Maginot, Minister of Pensions, a French soldier of the Verdun garrison laid a bunch of flowers upon one of the coffins. Placed on a gun carriage, the coffin was taken to the train station and placed on a train to Paris, where he was buried on 11 November 1920 in a prepared grave under the Arc de Triomphe. The seven remaining bodies were buried together in a French military cemetery. (The President of the Republic exercised his right of clemency in favour of 98 sailors and 2,781 soldiers, two of whom were under sentence of death.)

tion of war. They were the bereaved.

CROWDS IN THE STREETS.

GRIEF AND TRIUMPH.

He has passed, and the Empire, with bowed head, has paid its tribute. To every member of the vast crowd that assembled along the route the solemn cortege made a personal appeal. Was this the son, so long reported missing; the husband, or the comrade of the trenches? It mattered not, the appeal was equally strong. He might be there in the plain casket beneath the Union Jack. And there was, too, the wider symbolical meaning; it was the nation's homage to all who fell. Everywhere along the route the same deep feeling prevailed; everywhere the congregation was in harmony with the solemnity of the occasion. It was an unwonted demeanour for a London crowd, usually so spirited. Save for the very young, by one and all the full meaning was understood, and people either talked in subdued tones or remained silent.

The waiting moments were spent in thought rather than in conversation, and from beginning to end orderliness prevailed. Rarely can the police have had so light a task, for there was a general desire to co-operate in carrying out the regulations. The instructions regarding the barriers were strictly observed. In Trafalgar-square there was no unseemly rush when the gates were opened at 8.15, and even as late as nine o'clock the police in the neigh-

---

unduly heard in Whitehall, and appeared to echo and re-echo through the long and almost silent thoroughfare.

THE KING ARRIVES.

Sound of Distant Music as the Procession Approaches.

Well in advance of eleven o'clock the King and Queen with various other members of the Royal family drove to the Home Office, where the Royal ladies were conducted to positions assigned to them commanding a view of the cenotaph. The King, with his sons, the Duke of Connaught, and other male members of the Royal Family, passed through the buildings into Whitehall.

There was, of course, no cheering and no demonstration of any kind except that the various naval and military officers, already in position, saluted the King and were saluted by him in return. His Majesty wore the uniform of a Field Marshal, and, like all the other officers taking part in the ceremony, had a broad crepe band round one arm.

The Prince of Wales wore the uniform of a Colonel of the Welsh Guards, and with him were the Duke of York, in air force uniform, and Prince Henry, in military dress.

It was noticed that Colonel Wigram, Assistant Private Secretary to the King, was carrying a large wreath of bays and laurels entwined with red roses.

Lord Claud Hamilton, Equerry to the Prince of Wales, carried a very similar wreath, except that the relieving blooms in this [illegible] were white.

His Majesty took up a position immediately in front of the cenotaph on the Trafalgar Square side, near to a small erection fitted with an electrical apparatus for the removal of the huge Union Jacks with which the memorial was draped.

At about 10 45 the comparative silence was broken by the sound of distant music, and it was realised that the funeral procession had

---

owing to indisposition. dee.

TIME TABLE OF CENOTAPH AND ABBEY CEREMONIES.

The King's Leading Part in Solemn Tribute.

WAR SOIL ON COFFIN.

All arrangements for the solemn observance of Armistice Day are now complete.

The funeral procession bearing the remains of the Unknown Warrior starts from Victoria Station at 9.40 this morning. The route will be by way of Grosvenor-place, Grosvenor-gardens, Constitution-hill, the Mall, Admiralty Arch and Whitehall.

A Field-Marshal's salute of nineteen shots will be fired at Hyde Park by "N" Battery, R.H.A., as the coffin is lifted on to a gun carriage at the station. The cortege will be as follows:—

Bands and drums of the Foot Guards.
Pipers of the Scots Guards.
THE COFFIN
on a gun-carriage with the following pall-bearers:—
Admirals Sir Hedworth Meux, Lord Beatty, Sir Henry Jackson, General Albert Farrar-Gatliff, Sir Charles Madden, Field-Marshals Lord French, Lord Haig, Lord Methuen and Sir Henry Wilson, Generals Lord Horne and Lord Byng, and Air-Marshal Sir Hugh Trenchard.
Units of the Royal Navy.
Representatives of the Mercantile Marine.
Representatives of practically every unit in the Army.
The Royal Air Force representatives.
Ex-Service men's organisations.

Shortly before eleven o'clock the procession will reach the Cenotaph, which, on the stroke of the hour, will be unveiled by the King.

THE TWO MINUTES' HUSH.

---

with the thought of the past, with its glories and tragedies heavy upon them.

"UNFORGETTABLY IMPRESSIVE."

The sound of a Field-Marshal's salute of 19 guns from Hyde Park was the signal to the waiting thousands that the unknown had started on his last journey. A war-stained Union Jack covered the coffin, which was surmounted by the King's Crusader's sword and the webbing equipment and steel helmet of the British soldier. The coffin was placed upon a gun carriage, and before the order was given to proceed four wreaths of laurel and palm leaves were placed upon it—a tribute from our Allies in the Great War.

The pall bearers—Earl Beatty, Earl Haig, Sir Hedworth Meux, Lord French, Lord Horne, Lord Byng, and Air-Marshal Sir Hugh Trenchard—joint leaders of the men in the mighty struggle—took up their stations at the side of the carriage, and then amidst the salutes of the guns the cortege moved off, amidst the deeply impressive music of the massed bands and the roll of muffled drums.

As the procession wended its way between ranks of soldiers standing with bowed heads and arms reversed, with the vast crowds behind them, the pipers of the Scots Guards took up the funeral dirge, the shrill notes so expressive of war and of triumph seeming to accentuate the profound silence which otherwise prevailed.

Viewed from the roof of the Admiralty Arch, the scene as the cortege approached down the Mall was unforgettably impressive. A thick haze obscured Buckingham Palace and the Queen Victoria Memorial, and the arrival of the procession was only heralded by the rolling of the drums, above which could be heard the strains of Chopin's beautiful Marche Funebre.

AT THE CENOTAPH.

How the newspapers saw the events of 11 November 1920. Clockwise from top left: The Daily Telegraph; Manchester Evening News; Lancashire Daily Post, Daily Mirror.

The Western Front—Selected Areas of Interest

1. Mons—First British shot fired, 22 August 1914
2. Ypres—The scene of three battles
3. Calais Channel Port
4. Boulogne Channel Port
5. Etaples—The infamous British training area
6. Haig's Command HQ from 1916
7. St Pol—Where the body of The Unknown Warrior was selected
8. Albert area of the Somme: 1 July 1916
9. Vimy—Taken by Canadians, Easter Monday, 1917
10. Lille/Loos—area of the first British offensive, 1915
11. Cambrai—The first ever tank battle, November 1917
12. Compiègne—Where the Armistice was signed
13. River Marne—The furthest point of retreat of the Allied Armies, 1914
14. Versailles Treaty signed, 28 June 1919. Not to scale.

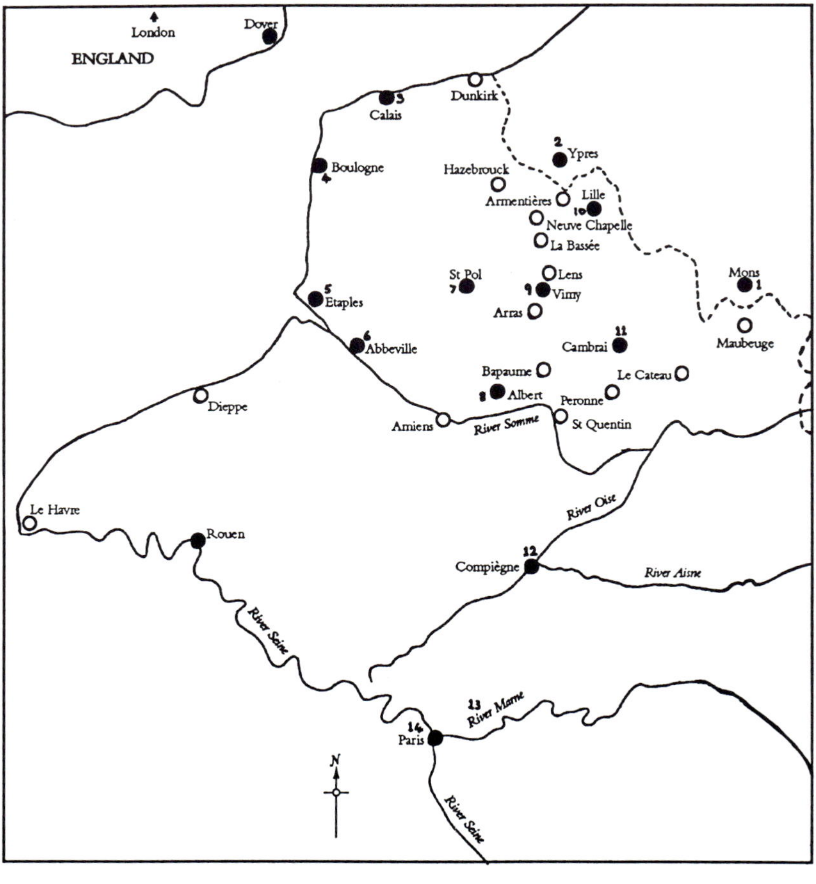

The Western Front: The battle areas from which the bodies were selected and actions fought

1. Ypres–Passchendaele
2. Arras–Loos/Neuve Chapelle, Vimy
3. Cambrai–Le Cateau, Mons
4. Somme, Thiepval, Serre, Pozieres
5. Aisne area—German offensive March, 1918
6. Marne—Furthest point of the Allied retreat

Not to scale

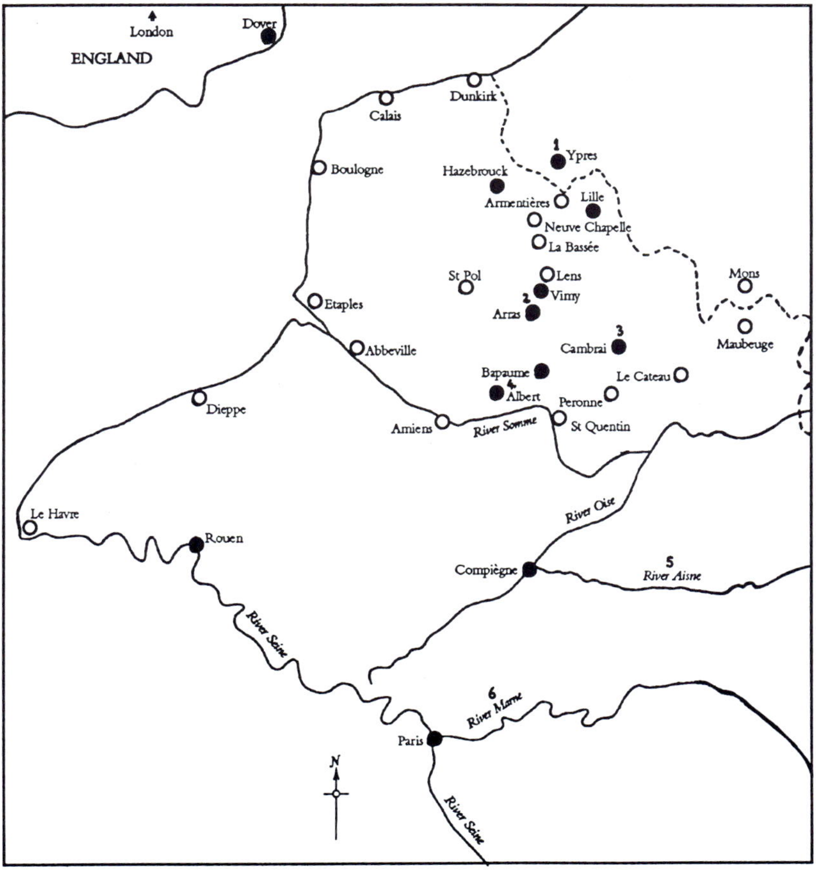

Route of the Unknown Warrior
St Pol–Boulogne–Dover–London
November 8, 9, 10 1920

Not to scale

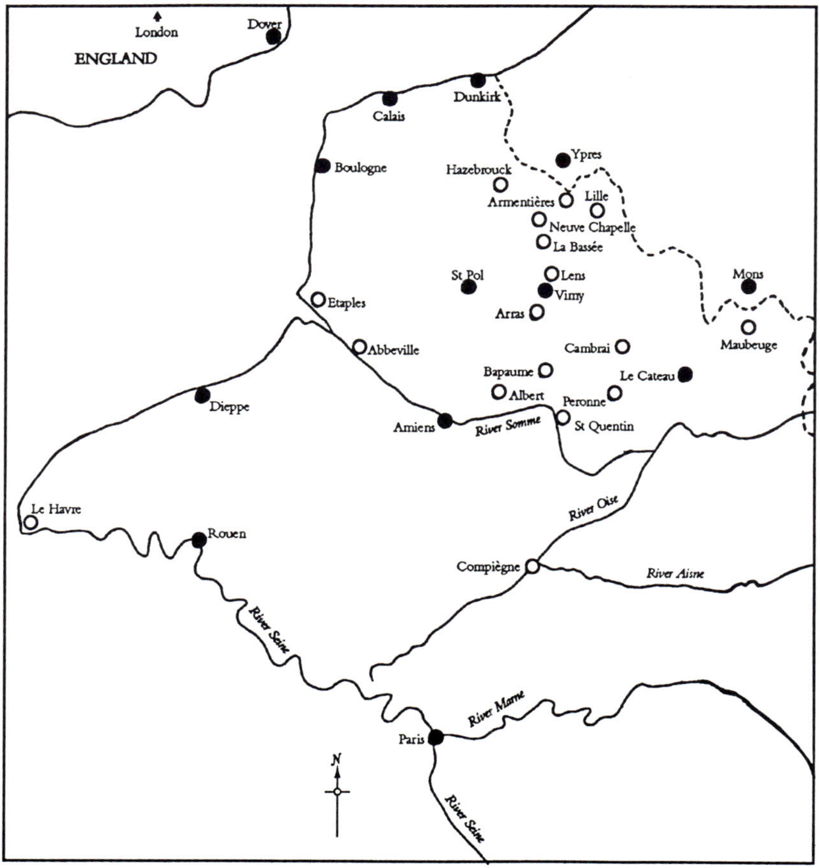

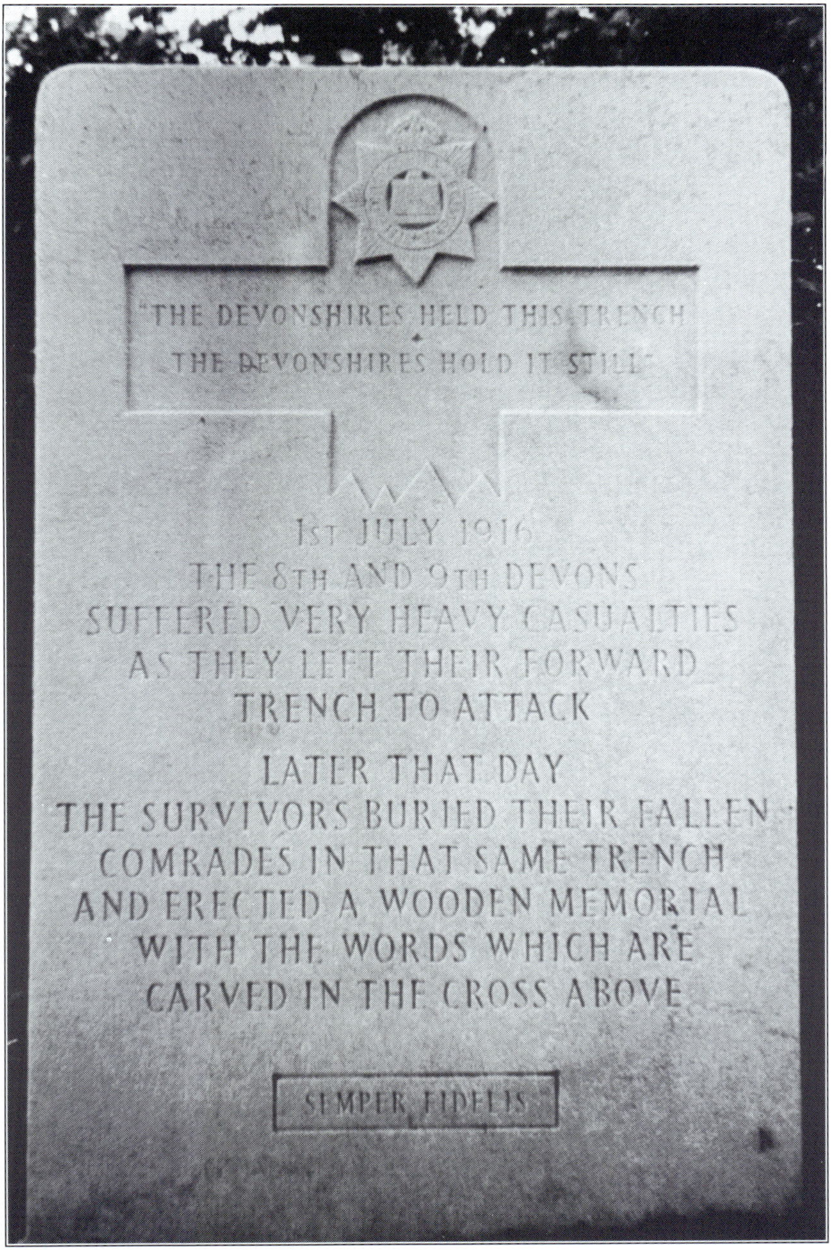

A poignant reminder. The Devonshire Trench, the Somme.
(Author.)

British dates of interest
World War I

1914

28 June	Assassination of Archduke Ferdinand and his wife in Sarajevo
4 August	Britain declares war on Germany
22 August	Pte Parr, 4 Middlesex, first British soldier killed in World War I
22 August	L/Cpl Thomas, 4th Royal Dragoons fires the first British shot of the war at Mons.
23 August	Lt Dease wins the first VC of the war at Mons (Royal Fusiliers), his parents received the medal by post in 1915. (Educated at Stonyhurst College)
8 September	First execution of a British soldier by Military Court-Martial
15 September	Battle of the Marne
17 September	Race to the Sea begins
12 October	First Battle of Ypres
8 December	The Naval engagement of the Falkland Islands

1915

10 March	Battle of Neuve Chapelle
22 April	Second Battle of Ypres begins
25 April	Gallipoli landings
9 May	Battle of Aubers Ridge
25 September	Battle of Loos
19 December	Gen. Haig replaces Sir John French as Commander in Chief of the British Army in France/Belgium

1916

24 April	Easter Rising in Dublin
	Turkey's army take Kut and capture the British Invasion Force
31 May/1 June	Battle of Jutland
1 July	Battle of the Somme commences 7.30 a.m. Saturday. Highest British loss of life in one day, over 19,000 dead, more than 38,000 wounded

1917

February	British Forces retake Kut.
21 May	Imperial War Graves Commission established by Royal Warrant.
31 July	Third Battle of Ypres (Passchendaele) commences.
20 November	Battle of Cambrai, first ever tank battle, (church bells sounded in England for the first time in the war)
11 December	Jerusalem falls to the British and Dominion troops

1918

21 March	German offensive against the Allies in France/Belgium
26 March	Marshal Foch appointed Commander Allied Armies.
1 April	Royal Air Force formed
18 July	Allied counter offensive begins
9 November	Kaiser Wilhelm II abdicates.
11 November	Pte Ellison was the last British soldier to be killed in the war
11 November	Armistice signed at Compiegne, north of Paris, in a railway carriage

Annex A
No. 1

6th November, 1920.

28/1371. A.G.4A.

Sir,

I am directed to inform you that the body of the "Unknown Warrior" will arrive at Dover at 15.30 hours on the 10th instant on the Destroyer, H.M.S. "Verdum". The body will be accompanied by the Adjutant General to the Forces, Lieut. General Sir G.M.W. Macdonogh, K.C.B., K.C.M.G.

1. A salute of 19 guns will be fired when the body is brought ashore.
2. The troops at Dover will parade to receive the body.

Will you therefore take steps to parade the Garrison between the landing place and the train or make such arrangements as may be most suitable and inform the War Office of your proposals.

A guard of one officer and 15 other ranks will be required to travel with the body from Dover to London, where the body will be handed over to a guard of the Brigade of Guards and the guard provided by the Eastern Command will return on completion of its tour of duty.

I am,

Sir,

Your obedient Servant,

(Signed) H. C. Sutton

Colonel

Deputy Director of Personal Services.

Head Quarters,

Eastern Command.

No. 2

M.43829/20.

ADMIRALTY, S.W.1.
6th November 1920.

The Commanding Officer,
H.M.S. "VERDUN".
(under cover to the Senior Naval Officer, Harwich)

I am to acquaint you that Their Lordships have selected H.M.Ship under your command to convey a coffin containing the remains of an Unknown Warrior from Boulogne to Dover on November 10th.

Departure from Harwich.

2.– Being in all respects ready for sea, H.M.S. "VERDUN" is to leave Harwich on November 9th, and is to arrive at Dover before dark that day. She is to leave dover on November 10th in time to enter Boulogne Harbour at 1000 on that day.

Arrival Boulogne

On arrival at Boulogne Harbour, H.M.S. "VERDUN" should be turned with bows to seaward and berthed at No.1 berth, Quai Chanzy. This is the Northern end of the Quai and the berth is in the occupation of the S.E. & C.Rly.Co., whose Marine Superintendent, Captain Blake, has made the necessary arrangements.

Embarkation of Coffin at Boulogne

4.– The coffin will be embarked by the Military when "VERDUN" has berthed. Lieutenant General Sir charles Macdonogh K.C.B., K.C.M.G., Adjutant General to the Forces will take over the body at Boulogne and will accompany it to Dover.

Expenses incurred in providing entertainment and comforts for the Guard of Honour may be reclaimed from the Accountant General.

Ceremony.

5.– The coffin is to be received on board H.M.S. "VERDUN" by a seamen guard of about 20 men under an officer, and placed on a bier in a suitable position. A large Union Jack is to be taken to cover the coffin from Boulogne to

London.

Colours to be half-masted as the coffin arrives on board. The ship's company is to be fallen in. After arrival on board, sentries with arms reversed are to be posted round the bier.

Departure

6.– H.M.S. "VERDUN" is to proceed to sea after embarking the coffin and should clear the berth not later than 1230 as it will be required by the Railway Company at that time.

Arrival at Dover

7.– After leaving Boulogne Harbour H.M.S. "VERDUN" is to cruise in mid channel as requisite, entering Dover Harbour in time to berth at No.3 berth Marine Station, at 1530, weather permitting.

Berthing

8.– The King's Harbour Master, Dover, is to give directions as to berthing, informing Commanding Officer and Military of any alterations necessary.

Disembarkation of coffin

9.– The coffin is to be conveyed on shore and turned over to Bearers for conveyance to the train.

General Directions

11.– H.M.S. "VERDUN" has been specially selected to perform this duty as a compliment to the French Nation. Special attention should therefore be paid to the appearance of ship and Ship's Company. The Officers should wear No.5 dress with swords and Mourning Bands, the men No.2.

The coffin is being brought over on 10th in order to avoid any accident on morning of 11th. It will be sent to London by train leaving Dover at 1750 and remain at Victoria for the night of the 10th.

Weather conditions prevailing during the passage may necessitate some modification in these orders at the discretion of the Commanding Officer.

W/T. Constant watch on 600 metres from time of leaving Harwich until return thereto.

The Commander-in-Chief, Nore has been requested to provide a 600 metre guard at Nore from 0400 to 1900 on November 10th.

Any message for the King's Harbour Master, Dover, can be passed on 300 metres to Folkestone Harbour W/T Station (call sign G.U.R.)

Pilotage at Boulogne. Pilotage is compulsory, in that a Pilot must be paid for whether taken or not.

Tug at Boulogne. One Tug has been ordered by S.E. & C.Rly. Co., to stand by, if required.

Reports. Arrival and departure at each port is to be reported to Admiralty, Commander-in-Chief Nore and Senior Naval Officer, Harwich.

Speed. To be as required.

Passengers. Two Undertakers will take passage in "VERDUN" from Boulogne to Dover. Their names are Sourbutts and Nodes. They will be furnished by Sir Lionel Earle with a letter of identification.

Care of Coffin. Suitable precautions should be taken to prevent any risk of damage in transit.

12.– The recept of these orders is to be acknowledged by telegram.

13.– Copies of these orders have been sent to the:-
Commander-in-Chief Atlantic Fleet
Rear Admiral (D)
Senior Naval Officer Harwich
Commander-in-Chief, The Nore
King's Harbour Master Dover.

BY COMMAND OF THEIR LORDSHIPS

(Signed) Alex Hint

No. 3

SECRET

(This Document is the Property of His Britannic Majesty's Government and should be returned to the Foreign Office if not required for official use)

FRANCE

POLITICAL

Decypher. Lord Derby. (Paris) November 9th 1920.
D. 8.15 p.m.
November 9th 1920
R. 10.40 p.m.
No. 1313.

Marshal Foch and General Weygand are proceeding to Boulogne to-night to do honour to body of unknown British Soldier on its departure from France. I would suggest that His Majesty's Government should send a message of thanks to Marshal Foch who has chosen to do this entirely on his own initiative.

C.2. Copies to:-

D.M.I. D.D.M.I.
M.I.3, 3a, 6.
A.G. D.P.S.
D.D.P.S. (A)
A.G.4.A.

Sources

Garnett, Richard, *The Final Betrayal* (1989).
Jeans, Herbert, 'In Death's Cathedral Palace (The Story of the Unknown Warrior)', *British Legion Journal* Vol 9 No 5, November 1929.
After the Battle No 6, 1974
Sier, E. C., 'How they chose the Unknown Warrior', *Reveille*, Sydney NSW, November 1967
Watrin, Janine, *The British Military Cemeteries in the Region of Boulogne-sur-Mer* (Book Club Ltd., 1977).
Blythe, Ronald, *The Age of Illusion* (Oxford University Press, 1983).
Hundeval, John, 'The Unknown Warrior', *The Legionary* Vol 30 No 3, August 1955.
Railton, the Reverend David, 'The Origins of the Unknown Warrior', *Our Empire* Vol VII 1931.
Tiddall, E. E. R., 'How they chose the Unknown Warrior', *British Legion* Vol 10, No 5, 1939.
The Daily Telegraph 9, 10, 11, 12 November 1920
The Daily Mirror 9, 10, 11, 12 November 1920
Dover News 10, 11 November 1920
Manchester Evening News 11 November 1920
Lancashire Evening Post 11, 12 November 1920
Daily Express 16 September 1919, 12November 1920
Williamson, Lt. Col., *The Daily Telegraph* 14 October 1993
Wyatt, Brigadier General, *The Daily Telegraph*, November 1939
Public Record Office, Kew, PRO WO3/3000
Imperial War Museum, London
Harris Museum and Library, Preston
Westminster Abbey, Muniment Room and Library
Dover Museum
The London Illustrated News
Liverpool Echo
Sir Cecil Smith, letter to Dean Carpenter.
Drinkwater, B., 'The Day they Buried the Unknown Warrior', *Picture Postcard Monthly*, November 1992.
Brazier, James, The Western Front Association Bulletin, due for publication October 1995.
Cave, T., 'The Unknown Warrior', WFA Bulletin No. 17, October 1986.
Combs, R., 'Before Endeavours Fade', *After the Battle*, published 1976.

Useful Addresses

Listed are addresses which are interesting places to visit and have been of assistance in compiling this story.

Westminster Abbey
London SW1P 3PA

Imperial War Museum
Lambeth Road
London SE1 6HZ

National Railway Museum
Leeman Road
York YO2 4XJ

Commonwealth War Graves
Commission (for enquiries)
2 Marlow Road
Maidenhead, Berkshire SL6 7DX

Dover Museum
Market Square
Dover, Kent CT16 1PB

Royal Naval Museum
Portsmouth, Hampshire PO1 3LR

Harris Library and Museum
Market Street
Preston, Lancashire

Public Record Office
Kew
Richmond, Surrey TW9 4OU

Guards Museum
Wellington Barracks
Birdcage Walk
London SW1E 6HQ

The Royal British Legion
49 Pall Mall
London SW1Y 5JY

Windsor Castle
Windsor
Berkshire SL4 1NG

Royal Engineers Library
Brampton Barracks
Chatham
Kent ME4 4UG

Royal Artillery Institution
Old Royal Military Academy
Woolwich
London SE18 4DN

Western Front Association
Membership Secretary
David Harrison
16 Conway Road
West Wimbledon
London SW20 8PA